MORE PRAISE FOR UNDER THREE HUNDRED WORDS

These letters, collected over two decades, give the reader a rich sense of how our country has changed–the consequences and now outcomes. The letters give a voice both responding to and resisting the unfolding history of the North Country of the Adirondacks.
—Marjorie Madigan, Professor Emerita of History, Marymount Manhattan College

These letters are an excellent example of cogent, acutely perceptive writing which analyze a wide span of current social issues. Moreover they articulate urgent interconnections relevant to the survival of a democratic society and a sustainable earth. For any person who cares about our world, they are well worth reading.
—Maida Solomon, historian, teacher, writer

Bernice weaves thoughts into comprehensible phrasing with thoughtful provoking questions.Her letters give voice to her community, engaging readers to understand their own responsibility from a place of truth and honesty, using a moral compass of respect for democratic principles, and stating actions for all to live by: "...to affirm love, peace, beauty, bounty, diversity, justice, interconnection and independence of and for all beings."
—Paula Sawyer, singer, living in and with the beauty of nature

As a devoted reader of Bernice's letters, I highly recommend this book. It carries on our commune's South Baltimore Voice written 50 years ago to give voice to our community.
—Margaret Blanchard, teacher, poet, novelist, artist

UNDER THREE HUNDRED WORDS

The new schoolyard bullies

Editor:

In the schoolyard there were always some bullies. I would see them strutting around and think (and sometimes say) "who are you, little big shots, bossing everyone around, yelling, threatening, making people afraid." I see and say the same words now to our present day bullies, the so called "freedom caucus" who want only freedom for themselves, who challenge every election they lose as rigged, who silence dissent and cast out anyone who does not spout the lie that the 2020 election was stolen or that the violent mob storming the capital were peaceful protestors and innocent hostages. They are the so called "mothers for liberty" banning books they've never read, attacking teachers, librarians, election workers doing their good work; they are in the Republican State legislatures demanding their extreme right wing laws be enacted, "inciting fear and stoking anger."

Frustrated by their antics, Republican Governor Mike Parson of Mississippi said, "This is unequivocally and without a doubt, the worst show of bad faith I have ever seen in my life."

They claim they're true Conservatives, all other Republicans RINO's. In reality they get their "script" from Trump and those wanting total power, "voting in lock-step in accordance with the message instructions they receive." Many Republican State Legislators frustrated by their antics are fed up with this "small group of swamp creatures trying to destroy institutions for their own selfish ambition." "They have bamboozled people into believing that their fiery rhetoric and their preference for anarchy is conservative...the reality is that they are an obstruction and an annoyance." They are our rabid legislator Stefanik, bombastic Gaetz, conspiracy theorists and MAGA Republicans in the House attacking Biden, impeaching Mayorkas, refusing to pass bills that protect our borders, aid Ukraine, or help average Americans... kowtowing to Trump, the biggest bully in our school yard.

Bernice Mennis
West Fort Ann

UNDER THREE HUNDRED WORDS

LETTERS TO A LOCAL NEWSPAPER

BERNICE MENNIS

WEST FORT ANN
NEW YORK

ISBN 979-8-9885726-9-5
Printed in the United States of America

All photographs property of the author.

Book design by Booksmyth Press
Shelburne Falls, MA

Dedicated
to the preservation of
Community
Democracy
Earth
Truth

INTRODUCTION: WHY THIS BOOK

It started with Bush and Cheney proclaiming "weapons of mass destruction" as a reason to overthrow Saddam Hussein and go to war in Iraq. It was clear there were no weapons, no need for war. Most people around the world protested, as did we, in Saratoga, in Glens Falls. Colin Powell spoke at the UN holding up something that looked like proof and the war began and continued for years– all the bravado, all the lies, all the deaths for no reason, a group of us gathering to protest for weeks and months… and I began to write letters to our local newspaper <u>The Post Star</u>, beginning what became a mild obsession to give voice to feelings: to write letters—two a month, each letter under 300 words, hundreds of letters.

My need to find a form for feelings started many years before–in teaching, in writing poetry and essays, in organizing for "causes "-- against war, for tenant rights, for the rights of women, for workers' rights, for environmental rights. I just found copies of the "South Baltimore Voice," newsletters written by our commune in Baltimore, 1971-2. And a long time before then, as a child growing up in the Bronx, seeing bullies in the school yard, teachers in public school demeaning students, people in power asserting superiority, people everywhere making racist, antisemitic, anti immigrant comments, and feeling fear in our Bronx immigrant neighborhood when McCarthy began rounding up "Communists" to testify before the "House of UnAmerican Activities," my almost instinctive response then (and now) was: "Who do you think you are anyway?"

On a psychological level, I am an "enthusiast" in my Enneagram test. I am flanked by "justice." I relate to those characteristics: the enthusiast who connects and reacts to the external world strongly– my deep appreciation and joy at goodness, kindness, courage, generosity, integrity--how deeply they touch my heart and inspire my spirit. And my anger at deliberate cruelty, intentional lies, violence, corruption, injustice, at what kills people and spirit. My letters capture those voices.

I think about what feels essential to our identity through all our years and all our changes. The poet William Stafford writes of the "thread one follows."

There's a thread you follow. It goes among
Things that change. But it doesn't change.
People wonder about what it is you are pursuing.
You have to explain about the thread.
But it is hard for others to see.
While you hold it you can't get lost.
Tragedies happen; people get hurt
Or die; and you suffer and get old.
Nothing you can do can stop time's unfolding.
You don't ever let go of the thread.

I see that thread–in my political actions, my essays, writing, teaching–
and in these letters to the editor of a local newspaper.   Now, at age 78, I
want to gather together the letters through the years, to slowly read them–to
hear my own thoughts and words and, also, see again the larger history
unfolding in our world, all that was occurring outside of me to which i felt
the need to respond. I wonder if I said the same thing again and again? Did
the same forces of power and greed and misinformation keep repeating,
although in different forms? And why, every month, did i feel compelled to
write to our local paper and to my local community.,

My first "answer": community. I love what is local, love the farmers'
market, buy from small local stores, always shun the big and corporate,
move to the small and familiar. I love where I have lived for forty four
years– the Adirondack mountains, our small home in the woodlands, feel
connected to "place"--the stream, spring, mountains, trees, plants, seasons.
I love the quiet of solitude of our woodlands. And i love the energy of
community.

And why write to this newspaper? Because it is local, because local
newspapers are disappearing, 2000 in the last decades, engulfed by
conglomerates, mainly controlled by those with money from far away,
not hearing or caring about the voices and lives of the community, often
having their own political agenda. Local newspapers, largely run by
families, providing a kind of factual accountability of place and time, have
been dying I can feel what is lost when they disappear: shared identities,
local news, farms, crops, weather, sports teams, voter information, candidates, stories of people living in the community, what is happening in the
schools and libraries, corruption on local levels, protests, balloon festivals, blueberries, strawberries, corn, Autumn's leaf colors, snow levels,
businesses closing, trees affected by invasive species, water quality, workers

organizing, proposed legislation, regulations about pesticides, debates over spending–issues small and large. Even if we disagree with opinions and editorials, local papers make us think, tell us what we may not know, help us feel connected to our community.

The Post Star, our local newspaper, gets smaller and smaller. There are reductions in staff and in content, Recently it was reduced to printing only three days a week and the rest digital. It may not be able to survive, and that would be a loss. They say that when local newspapers fold, local corruption increases, polarization gets stronger. Small towns, small businesses get lost in globalization. HIghtower, in his August 10 newsletter, writes: "The demise of local newspapers has been a very depressing story in the last few years with several thousand of them gobbled up by Wall Street profiteers– moneyed powers which loot the publications' assets, then callously shut down each community's paper or reduce them to empty shells ..." But, and this is the good news according to Hightower, "High spirited community-minded subscribers in places like Glen Rose (Texas), Hamburg (Iowa), Portland (Maine) and International Falls (Minnesota)" are humming an upbeat tone of regeneration"-- In Maine "National Trust for local news" bought the failing daily newspapers and turned them over to local nonprofit owners; the Cherry Road Media bought 77 rural papers in l7 states from the predatory Gannett conglomerate to return editorial decisions to local people and reinvest profits in local journalism. We need to find out more…about how to return and turn our communities to democracy." I think of our very local "South Baltimore Voice" and the need to return.

Letters themselves are almost a relic of the past in our quick moving digital age: with text messages, short emails, pods and blogs, with our addiction to technology, to speed, efficiency, we insisting that people respond immediately, hardly using sentences, everything abbreviated, everything an emergency, the bombardment of information….I spoke to someone yesterday who told me that she had to teach her 20 years old daughter how to sign her own name because they stopped teaching cursive, a skill we all learned and practiced so diligently in grammar school. What does that loss mean in terms of our connecting to all or any of our senses–to our hand writing on a sheet of paper? I continually think of the need to measure "cost" (and loss) in our quest for "progress" and "growth."

I taught for many years at a progressive school in Vermont. Students met once a month. They would read many books, would write long essays and poetry, would mail me their work, and I, in silence and solitude, would read their words, written in silence and solitude, and return long letters responding to their thoughtful work. There was no sense of urgency, no need to get a quick response. What was needed then and now was space and quiet to think, to silently reflect. I became a letter writer to my students, to my friends, to my community, and, then, to my local newspapers, mostly to the editor of *The Post Star.*

> But words are things, and a small drop of ink falling like dew upon a thought, produces that which makes thousands, perhaps millions, think. (Lord Byron)

Gathering information, quotes, poems, researching history, facts, stories. I began to write letters that I hoped would allow thinking, learning, questioning, would deepen awareness and possibly action, hoping for the awakened "now I see."

> Not everything that is faced can be changed, but nothing can be changed unless it is faced. (James Baldwin)

As a teacher, I could understand the fear that imprisons us, restricting our inner and outer explorations, and would try to create a safe space for vulnerability, openness, honesty, for taking risks. I sometimes distributed the following poem, "Litany for Survival," where Audre Lorde talks about "the illusion of safety" by which the "heavy footed hoped to silence us." She talks of the fear and the need to speak:

> …"and when we speak we are afraid/
> our words will not be heard
> nor welcomed
> But when we are silent
> We are still afraid
> So it is better to speak
> Remembering
> we were never meant to survive."

The joy, the freedom of speaking what has been silenced, the necessity for us and our world.

Since writing this introduction I have written more letters.. I realize that the process of thinking of writing, of giving form to feeling will go on and on. Last night i could not sleep, fearing for my country, my world, our earth, fearing that the power of money to control and shape our thoughts, the misinformation and conspiracy theories, the forces of hatred, propaganda, the ignorance… will go on and on, as they have throughout the centuries.

But what is also true was that people of good will and care will also go on and on, courageous people working to save our earth and our democracy, risking their lives. I thought of poems that persevere through years and centuries, that continue to speak, thought of Auden's "September 1, 1939" where "the clever hopes expire on a low dishonest decade," and where "waves of anger and fear circulate over the bright and darkened lands of the earth." Auden writes of "what dictators do, the elderly rubbish they talk," "the windiest militant trash." Exactly what i feel now.

Auden writes "All i have is a voice/to undo the folded lie"and ends his poem with these words:

" Defenseless under the night
 Our world in stupor lies
 Yet, dotted everywhere,
 Ironic points of light
 Flash out wherever the Just
 Exchange their messages;
 May I, composed like them of Eros and of dust,
 Beleaguered by the same
 Negation and despair,
 Show an affirming flame."

And that, I think, is why I write, perhaps obsessively, without any real expectation of having an effect: "May I show a small affirming light."

Last night I went to art openings, beautiful creative work by people in my community. I was on the street with lights for local candidates wanting to make a difference in our community, candidates who could and would listen to the voices of people and their needs. I walked through the park by the library and saw the most beautiful leaves of red and gold and yellow, leaves whose shapes I did not recognize. I gathered them and pressed them in a book because they were so beautiful, as is so much of our world, and showed them to everyone I saw, saying "look, look, at the incredible bounty and beauty of our earth forever giving." Perhaps my letters have the same childlike and real feeling of "look, look, look."

Tonight I have an art show with a dear friend with whom I have been painting for decades. It is a big occasion worthy of celebration for us and what we love and what we do. So small, but still how good to celebrate any gesture of beauty and life.

Right now, early in the morning, the rain has just started. Beautiful rain in our beautiful woods where the leaves have begun to fall and will continue to fall. Each season, each letter, each reality of all of our lives giving form to feelings, doing what we can in our small lives. The art show tonight is called "Bounty."

October 7th 2002
Threat to freedom is power in hands of few

I am writing in love of democracy and freedom and in fear of what is happening now in our country, not about the enemies outside of us but the danger within.

The old story is how Bush became president, a recent court case revealing that 95,000 people in Florida were disqualified from voting because they might possibly be felons, Jeb Bush and Kathryn Harris stopping the procedure which would have brought the list of felons down to 3,000. Bush was "appointed" by the Supreme Court, not voted in. The more recent story of erosion of our democracy has to do with our attorney general who, instead of protecting our liberties, has expanded surveillance over American citizens in libraries, wants to establish a tips program where neighbors spy on neighbors, and has announced plans for camps for US citizens deemed "enemy combatants." When questioned, Ashcroft simply spoke of "the president's absolute authority in a time of war."

Our economy is worsening. Our national surplus is now a deficit. The percentage of poor has increased, workers are laid off, the stock market is plummeting, people can't afford adequate medical coverage, basic social services are being slashed. President Bush's tax cut benefited the most wealthy 1 percent. Major corporations have legal "Bermuda tax loopholes" and receive huge subsidies from our government. It is not just the corruption of "the few bad eggs" but the erosion of the power of the SEC to review such corruption and the deregulation of companies, first under Reagan and then under Gingrich's "securities reform" (passed over Clinton's veto).

Instead of building our economy, the president's "solution" is to call for war. Iraq is a good "target" because it has oil. Clearly, Iraq is a dictatorship and its leader a tyrant, but the United States has supported tyrants around the world. And when Cheney was CEO of the oil field supply firm Halliburton, his company did $23.5 million in business deals with Hussein under two subsidiaries, actually helping to rebuild this dictator's war damaged oil fields.

There are no links between al-Qaeda and Iraq and Iraq does not threaten the United States' security. What threatens our security, freedom and democracy and what threatens our entire world is the amassing of power in the hands of the very few in our government who ignore its citizens, silence its Congress, and act against the wishes of the international community.

February 19th, 2003
Keep leaders' actions in clear perspective

In "Propaganda Under a Dictatorship," Aldous Huxley gives a formula for how to separate people from reason and morality: Repeat a slogan over and over ("weapons of mass destruction"); view the world only in black and white, allowing no complexity ("axis of evil"); juxtapose ideas without proving any cause and effect (Iraq and al Qaeda); give no publicity to countering opinions (the 300,000 who marched in Washington against war as well as millions around the world); create a climate of fear, labeling all opposition unpatriotic.

I think of Germany during the 1930s, those who believed in their dictator and their nation and those who watched in fear and powerlessness. Some undisputed facts: It was the United States that supported Iraq in its war against Iran, supplying it with missiles and seed ingredients for biological warfare, doubling our military support "after" Saddam committed terror against his people. Perhaps it is the receipt for the weapons we sold him that constitute our "proof" that he has "weapons of mass destruction." During the Gulf War, we devastated the Iraqi weapons system and economy; there is nothing in these last 11 years that indicates any immediate danger from Saddam Hussein. The weapons inspection has found nothing.

It is so strange to me that our country, the most powerful nation in the world, is accusing Iraq of having weapons of mass destruction and of threatening America. Meanwhile, we have threatened to fire 300 missiles at them — on civilians, on people living their lives in their own country — on the first day of war causing "shock and awe." And we are threatening Germany and France that if they don't engage in this war against Iraq they will not share in the spoils of victory–all the rich oil fields we have already begun to divide.

A few random headlines in the Feb. 5 New York Times: "President Bush's budget proposes new eligibility requirements that would make it more difficult for low income families to obtain a range of government benefits from tax credits to school lunches." "Estimates of state budget deficits for the current fiscal year have grown by nearly 50 percent creating the worst fiscal outlook since World War II." The budget released recently projects a record deficit of about $304 billion." Some will get very rich but most of the world will feel the terrible cost.

18

June 8th, 2003
Government keeps letting us down

I know that the Republicans see themselves as fiscal conservatives who want government out of people's business; some actually may believe what they say. What I see, however, is a strong contradiction between image and reality. It is our current administration which has created a huge federal deficit having inherited a budget surplus (similar to Bush's creating a deficit in Texas having inherited former Texas Gov. Ann Richards' surplus).

True, this administration has consistently removed funds and services that help the poor and working people, but our government continues to increase its "subsidies" to huge corporations, funding Lockheed Martin and many companies here and abroad. (Look where our hard-earned tax dollars will go as we fund the oil and military companies "restructuring" the Iraq that we have just devastated–to the Haliburtons and Bechtels from which 35 members of our present administration receive direct economic gains.)

It is true that last year I received a tax return of $300 from the federal government, but I know that the very wealthy have received much more in huge tax benefits and companies are actually receiving millions of dollars back from taxes paid between 1992 and the present.

Meanwhile, almost every state budget is in shambles; schools are receiving less funds (so that many children are "left behind"); more people do not have medical coverage, unemployment continues to rise, housing and community health programs are being cut, there is less protection for our air and water and wildlife, the media is being concentrated in the hands of the very few, our civil liberties are being slowly eroded under the illusion of security.

What I don't understand is why people believe the words of this administration, untruths that are continually exposed and then fabricated anew. It does not "protect the forests" when we allow unrestricted clearcutting; we do not have "fresh air" when we lower emission standards; we do not create more jobs when we give more tax benefits to the very wealthy; we do not get rid of "weapons of mass destruction" when we, ourselves, begin to build a new nuclear arsenal

We need to look at their words and the actual reality--to question, to research, to look at our own experience, to rethink freedom and democracy, fiscal responsibility and the role of government, to understand what really makes our lives full and our country great.

August 26th, 2003
Reader calls for care in use of resouces

Many people, including our president, talk of the recent blackout as a "wake-up call." It was. But the new energy bill feels more like a call to sleep than to awareness.

It asks for more deregulation of the electrical industry (and the great cost to citizens), for taxpayer subsidization of nuclear energy (and the grave danger of accidents or terrorism), and for yet more drilling in the Arctic Wildlife Preserve. The "argument" is that we need more energy and that we should be able to have whatever we need, whenever we want it.

I think of Robert Moses, New York City's Highway Commissioner, who kept building more expressways. As each new expressway became more congested, he would propose yet another one, destroying one neighborhood (which he saw as a slum) after another until he was finally stopped by a community in Lower Manhattan. I think of that with our energy consumption: There will never be "enough"; the more we use, the more we will need.

The United States has 4 percent of the world's population, yet we use 30 percent of the world's energy and emit into the atmosphere 25 percent of the carbon dioxide. It is unfair and unjust.

Congress last year voted down legislation requiring automakers to produce vehicles capable of an average of 35 miles per gallon and, instead, actually gave incentives to buy big gas guzzlers. President Bush rejected the Kyoto Protocol requiring industrial nations to reduce emissions of CO_2 and gasses that contribute to global warming. His new energy plan would actually increase the carbon output by 23 percent; his "clear skies" initiative would cause a 50 percent increase in emissions of sulfur dioxide, add millions of tons of nitrogen oxides, offer no new control for carbon dioxide, and increase the Northeast's devastating acid rain.

For our children and children's children, we do need to wake up. Our air, water and earth are precious, irreplaceable and vulnerable. They are our life. We need to find alternative and sustainable energy resources and be responsible stewards (rather than destroyers) of our good Earth

November 14th, 2003.
U.S. has embarked upon the wrong course

The core of all ethics, I believe, resides in our human heart: our ability to put ourselves in another's place, to walk in his/her moccasins for one mile before we judge. The Golden Rule flows from that empathy: to love our neighbor as ourselves. Perhaps more necessary than loving our neighbor (who is like us) is to love someone not like us. The Old Testament admonishes: "The stranger that sojourneth with you shall be unto you as the homeborn among you, and you shall love him as yourself because you, also, were a stranger in the land of Egypt."

Recently I saw an old newsreel of world reaction after Sept. 11. The streets in Europe and Asia and Africa were filled with people weeping, carrying signs in sympathy and love. I was very moved. A small African village actually offered 24 cows to the families of the victims, poor people who "loved" this "stranger" who resided in the most wealthy and powerful nation in the world.

Now millions hate and fear us. Why? Our self-image is that we are very generous. It's true we are the largest exporter of weapons, but in terms of economic aid, we give a smaller percentage of our GNP to poor countries than any "advanced" nation. We have shown a disdain for the world, beginning with Bush's refusal to sign the Kyoto protocol limiting emissions causing global warming. We have withdrawn or refused to sign international treaties, whether banning land mines or supporting women and children's rights or allowing inspectors access to U.S. prisoners of war (Geneva Conventions) or joining the World Court of Law. And we have attacked and now militarily occupy a sovereign nation despite the will of the United Nations and the large majority of the international community. Why?

There were no weapons of mass destruction; Iraq (as terrible and despotic it was)posed no threat to the United States. Our safety has not increased but diminished. The cost of our disconnection from others is high: their lives; our lives; $1 billion for just one day of bombs over Baghdad; another $87 billion now needed; every state government impoverished with cuts in education, health, community services.

Many view us with fear and hatred–an arrogant stranger with no heart, no empathy, no understanding of self or others.

March 26th, 2004
Presidential Consistency

I have been thinking about "consistency," a trait admired in our president.

It is true he has been totally consistent: tax breaks for the very wealthy, no inheritance tax, subsidies for corporations that outsource. He has consistently fought against raising the minimum wage, extending unemployment, compensation for overtime, benefits for veterans, affordable housing, and alternative energy. He has cut regulatory committees protecting consumers from corporate crimes and environmental infractions, consistently rewarding his friends in oil, armaments, timber and coal with key positions.

Bush as president has been totally consistent with Bush as governor: inheriting a healthy surplus from his predecessors and bringing Texas and our country to fiscal disaster.

His greatest consistency, however, is in his continual lies-about weapons of mass destruction and the need for war, the surplus and the tax cuts, the cost of the Medicare bill, and all the costs we will all pay for years to come.

There is no integrity in a consistency that silences opposition, distorts facts, and refuses to listen to informed economists, scientists, world leaders and its own citizens.

Consistency that is closed to reality is, at best, ignorance. At worst, it is fundamentalism and fascism.

7 September 13th, 2004
Both parties demand an end to Bush policy

It's strange to hear about "compassionate conservatism" and then read the extreme rightwing Republican platform, hear attacks filled with hatred and lies, and think of the last four years: an unnecessary war with its terrible costs and economic policies benefiting the very wealthy and giving nothing to most of us. I can't believe anyone would want "another four years." I was, therefore, pleased to hear Republicans and Conservatives speak out against the extreme right-wing takeover of their party.

Democrats want "to take our country back"; conscious and compassionate Republicans and conservatives also want to take their party back. They see the grave danger of this administration's policies: the huge deficit, erosion of constitutional rights, extreme right-wing judges, bogus science and limitations on medical research. They fear, as I do, the incredible power of the wealthy corporations, rigid "religious" fundamentalists, and those who would destroy democracy "in order to make us safe."

This administration has intimidated those who question their misguided policies. It's heartwarming when people—whatever their party—speak and vote for honesty, integrity, fiscal responsibility, a sane foreign policy, protection of our environment, and preservation of our Constitution, people who speak, despite intimidation, for wisdom and compassion.

May 1st, 2005
Republicans use filibusters, too

This administration won by a tiny margin, yet rules as if it has the right to control the world, feeling outraged with any opposition to its extreme policies. It has undermined our gains in terms of people's real needs in the workplace, in education, in the environment, in health and welfare.

All we have to do is look at our land and school taxes, our medical and educational system, our lack of affordable housing, at acid rain, polluted air, poisoned water. What has been totally consistent is their ability to lie, to call what they do "good" and to call everyone who opposes them "bad." We hear their now campaign to end the 200 year old filibuster in the Senate, acting as if opposition to their total control of all branches of our government is an act against God and religion.

The reality is that under the eight years of Clinton's presidency, the Republican Senate totally stalled the judicial process, allowing an enormous number of open positions for Bush to inherit. The Senate has already approved more than 200 of Bush's appointments, using the filibuster in very few cases. The judges are so extreme that even the American Bar Association has found them wanting

These proposed judges are on record for opposing the minimum wage, the 40-hour work week, and all environmental protection. They, not those who oppose them, are the extreme and partisan ideologues who would impose their will on us. It is very important to protect our real values and to fight against those who threaten democracy and our way of life. This administration– in its desire to impose its extreme agenda– is a real threat.

September 23rd, 2005
We shouldn't waste our natural resources

I saw a bumper sticker "Stop Global Whining." I hear the administration saying that there should be no blaming. But using reason and taking responsibility aren't whining or blaming; they are attempts to act thoughtfully.

In my classroom, I teach students how to think: to observe closely, raise questions, notice patterns, make connections, understand cause and effect. Europe, seeing the effect of auto emission on global warming and that the supply of oil was being depleted, built small energy efficient vehicles; it was common sense. In the U.S. we built gas guzzlers, refused to sign the Kyoto treaty, passed an energy bill subsidizing the already huge profits of oil companies and provided only tiny amounts for alternative and sustainable energy. Global warming means warmer waters, means more hurricanes, just as acid rain means dead fish and mercury means poison.

Some things are pretty simple: If we poison our earth, water and air, we poison our earth, water, and air. If we consume vast amounts of oil, we will, in the future, pay high gas prices and run out of oil; it is not a renewable resource. The good news is also the bad news: Our actions have effect; we reap what we sow. We can call legislation "healthy forests" and "clean air" as we destroy forests and poison the air. We can kill the messenger of bad news and call him a whiner or biased. We can, as 5 percent of the world, use one-third of the world's resources and contribute to half of the world's pollution. But what is real is real. The only question is whether we choose to be conscious or ignorant.

January 29th, 2006
Activities threaten our democracy

In airports and trains, there are signs to report any suspicious or dangerous activities to the authorities.

As a concerned citizen worried about dangerous activity, I would like to report the following: secret prison camps; torture and the refusal to abide by the Geneva Convention; disregard of international laws, bans, and treaties; a preemptive war based on lies and misinformation; surveillance of private citizens without judicial review; statements claiming the executive branch above law; secret changes and omissions to scientific and government documents about the toxic effects on environment and health; withdrawal of funds to agencies that regulate dangers to miners, workers, citizens; silencing and firing of those in the CIA, NSA, FDA, EPA who speak about government wrongdoing.

More basic, perhaps, I'd like to report a terrible epidemic: Greed–CEOs making 400 to 800 times what workers make, while workers lose jobs, pension plans, wages and medical benefits and people go hungry: a Medicare "reform" that is a feast for drug and insurance companies; an appropriation bill that gives more tax breaks to the wealthiest 1 percent and cuts Medicaid, student loans, and food stamps; bribes and terrible corruption in government so that our children's birthright – our fragile environment, our wilderness, national parks and forests – is given away to oil and mining interests.

I fear we are losing our compassion, our fundamental morality: to feed the hungry, clothe the poor, welcome the stranger, do unto others as we would have them do unto us.

Benjamin Franklin said, "Those that would give up essential liberty in pursuit of a little temporary security deserve neither liberty nor security." As citizens, we need to be aware of this grave danger and report those in "authority" whose activities threaten our safety, democracy and freedom.

March 15th. 2006
History can teach us dangers of leadership

In Abu Ghraib and Guantanamo secret prisons; here illegal, warrantless surveillance of citizens. This administration first denies, then goes after "whistleblowers," and then proclaims its right to absolute power in time of war. All of the above should outrage and frighten us.

I can understand why extremely wealthy individuals and huge corporations support this administration; they are making enormous profits. What I don't understand is why those who are losing jobs, pensions, heating aid, food assistance, student loans, and the protection of our environment and of a democratic country support this "czar."

Perhaps those in power understand psychology. In the Nuremberg Trial, Hermann Goering said: "The people can always be brought to the bidding of the leaders. All you have to do is tell them they are being attacked and denounce the pacifists for lack of patriotism and for exposing the country to danger. It works the same in every country."

Our country is less safe now from outside terrorism and also from inside repression. A nurse in a VA hospital is being investigated by the FBI for sedition for writing her newspaper about increasing cases of trauma in veterans.

Many Russian peasants found the wrong "enemy." If we support those who harm us, we may harm those who would really protect us.

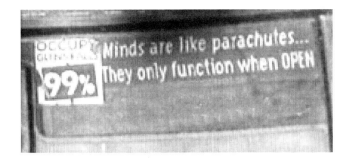

July 9th, 2006
Questioning those in power

I can understand why they repeat their familiar tactics: calling those who want to end our occupation of Iraq "cut and run" weak wimps; labeling those who protest the government's actions "unpatriotic"; bringing up the "marriage amendment" and condemning the burning of flags. What I don't understand is why those tactics work. Is it being strong and brave to arrogantly defend the indefensible? We now know we were lied to. There were no weapons of mass destruction; no link to 9/11.

What is clear is that we went to establish permanent bases and make business deals for oil, not to establish freedom; Iraqis and our soldiers are suffering and want us out. And is marriage so fragile it is endangered by someone wanting to make a lifetime commitment to a beloved of the same sex? And is patriotism so limited it doesn't include democracy, freedom and dissent? This administration calls those who expose torture, secret prisons, illegal spying, surveillance in libraries, on phones, in banks "disgraceful." What is disgraceful are not the courageous whistleblowers, but those who commit illegal abusive acts condemned by human rights groups and much of the world, acts that make us more hated and less safe.

We need to redefine courage, patriotism and morality; to look at actions, not just words. Who has actually served our country in the military and who sends others to do battle? Who votes to raise the minimum wage, aid veterans, protect workers and our environment and who consistently votes to benefit the wealthiest individuals and the largest corporations? Who raises his/her voice for ethics and who is involved with corporate scandal and greed? It is important to be subjects of our own precious lives, not objects manipulated by others. We need to question rather than to unthinkingly obey those who abuse power.

December 28th, 2007
Choose peace, justice for our fragile nation

This is the repeated nightmare that keeps me from sleep. We see an "enemy" that is "evil," we equate him with Hitler, we find "evidence" that this despot will develop weapons of mass destruction that threaten the world; we dismiss all contrary evidence from U.N. inspectors; we refuse to negotiate; we go to war.

So it was with Iraq falsely linking Saddam with 9/11, presenting "incontrovertible proof," disregarding world opinion, assuring everyone of the "enduring freedom" of "mission accomplished." Six years later Iraq is devastated, over a hundred thousand civilians have been killed, millions are fleeing. Civil war rages; we are hated, and terrorism increases around the world. We have spent billions of dollars creating harm instead of good. Now, learning nothing, we are ready to bomb Iran.

I shake my head in disbelief--secret prisons and "extraordinary rendition," sanctioned torture, denial of habeas corpus, wiretapping. Immunity for those who have committed crimes (Blackwater's killing innocent Iraqis, Internet companies illegally revealing names of customers), billions of dollars in corruption, continual lying in high office, scientific reports changed, people fired for not toeing the party line. We have restarted the Cold War with our bogus missile shield program and refused to join other nations in fighting global warming, banning landmines, establishing a world court. It is lonely to stand alone in the world. I would love to awaken from this nightmare to a vision of what is possible with consciousness and compassion. We have the money. The question is whether we choose life or death. It is not naive to recognize cause and effect, to negotiate with others, to limit our addictive consumption, to restrain greed, to recognize the interdependence of all beings, to protect our only and fragile earth, to choose peace and justice.

March 29th, 2008
Who should be impeached for crimes

One could go crazy thinking about who is in prison and who is "free." I taught in prison for 12 years and saw many serving long terms for possessing small amounts of drugs, robbing $700, being in a car with someone who left to commit robbery. I watched while those who had robbed millions keep their wealth—heads of Enron, savings and loan corporations, mortgage companies. Witnessed corporations that destroyed whole villages—gas leaks by Union Carbide killing 20,000 in India, Coca Cola poisoning drinking water, toxic waste destroying farmland—growing more prosperous. I think about which crimes rouse our virulent hatred and which go unpunished.

Spitzer was arrogant, Clinton foolish; both did wrong, but the harm was limited. But here is an administration that purposely lied about weapons of mass destruction and the connection between 9/11 and Iraq and led us into an immoral and disastrous war gone on for five years at enormous cost: one million Iraqis and 4,000 American soldiers dead, the financial cost $6 billion, with a total projected of $3 trillion. This administration has created world fear and instability and robbed Americans of future health care, environmental protection, education, job creation and training. Our taxes go to death, not life. They have sanctioned torture, secret prisons, denial of

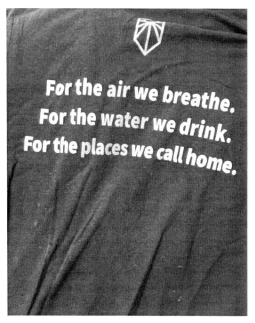

For the air we breathe. For the water we drink. For the places we call home.

habeas corpus and surveillance of its citizens, costing us all respect abroad. On today's news (March 20) I heard Bush speak of our victory because Iraqis can actually walk the streets and shop.

Before we invaded, people walked the street, went to school, went to museums, had electricity and led full lives. The vast majority of Iraqis want us out. Most Americans feel this war a mistake. I want these criminals in jail, impeached for their grave crimes against the world.

June 7th, 2008
Americans need to be open, not accusatory

You can't keep calling all who disagree with you unpatriotic, biased, politically motivated, disgruntled, left wing, evil or crazy. If the military criticizes this war, its inception and execution, if scientists speak of government documents changed to deny scientific facts, if those in the forest service, CIA, FBI, NASA and FDA reveal illegal practices, if judges are fired for not bowing to political pressure, if senate hearings expose lies, if newspapers finally reveal truths--at some point this administration needs to stop accusing and start listening.

We all have the capacity to deny what we do not want to hear. Name calling is easy in the school yard or in politics. When those in power name-call and use power to silence and threaten, we move from democracy to fascism.

To hold tightly to opinions by ignoring reality is not integrity, it is ignorance. And it is dangerous. Voltaire said, "Those who can make people believe absurdities can make them commit atrocities." I think of the many absurdities and atrocities: invading Iraq, a country that neither threatened us nor had any connection to 9/11; spending trillions for this war while cutting food stamps, education, job training, veteran benefits, medical programs, public broadcasting; being the only democracy without universal health care; giving huge subsidies to oil companies making record profits and cutting incentives for alternative energy, CEOs making 450 times a worker's salary; an Environmental Protection Agency fighting against clean air and water and an attorney general fighting against habeas corpus and justifying wiretapping and torture.

This is "crazy". It's difficult to open ourselves to information and facts that contradict cherished beliefs, but that is the only way to grow as individuals and as a society It is the choice to be conscious rather than arrogant, humble rather than righteous.

July 27th, 2008
Drilling for more oil will not solve issues

I think of Robert Moses' obsession with building more and more roads in New York City. Each time a new road would get congested, his solution was to build another road, devastating one community after another until finally stopped. Einstein said we cannot solve a problem using the same thinking that created that problem. More roads do not reduce city congestion, but rather create more traffic. And more drilling will not give us cheap oil and gas. Oil is a limited resource. When there is addiction, one does not give an addict more and more: lifting bans on offshore drilling, opening the Arctic National Wildlife Reserve, mining more coal (without clean technology), requiring ethanol use for fuel (not only not saving oil but driving up the price of food).

The problem with water is even more serious. In many countries, women and children walk miles for water and many die because of its lack. In parts of the U.S., water sources are being drained and in grave danger, yet we continue to have huge industrial farms, golf courses in the desert, and corporate industries polluting and depleting the waters of poor countries.

Privatization of water is not the answer. There are wars for oil and will be wars for water. For a while the powerful will have more, and the powerless will die. But there is a reality apart from greed and power. There is a limited carrying capacity for every area. We need to listen to the earth rather than demand it listen to us, need an ethic that recognizes the need to protect and preserve our waters, a will to find alternative and sustainable sources of energy, and an intelligence that recognizes the interdependence of all beings on earth. We need to "live simply so others can simply live."

September 19th, 2008
Republicans defying true religious morality

Recently the Pope spoke about the sin of "insatiable greed." Holy books speak of peace on Earth; doing unto others as we would have others do unto us; welcoming the stranger, feeding the hungry, clothing the poor; acting with kindness, honesty, respect, love.

How, I wonder, did morality get so reduced to no same-sex marriage, no abortion?

People are losing jobs and homes, food prices are rising and pantries are empty, people can't heat homes, drive to work or get medical help, how, morally, could one give large subsidies to oil companies making record profits, vote repeatedly against raising the minimum wage and protecting unions, refuse to raise taxes on the insatiably wealthy and not seek universal health care?

How is a teenager having a child cheered without asking if the mother is capable of raising that child, if the father is mature, ready for fatherhood? I, too, think of "family values," allowing mature people who have lived together in a committed way to marry and raise children; supporting parents who love their gay children; recognizing the rights of a woman to choose her life.

How is it that thinking deeply is scoffed at as elitist?   How is denial of reality, banning books, negating science and denying people information which enables them to make conscious choices "Christian?" What is really pro-life, pro-family, conservative? What are the fundamentals of all religions?

December 29th, 2009
U.S. is acting like a big global bully

Some issues are complex. But as children we knew what was fair or unfair, just or unjust. We could see who were the bullies taking over the field.

I think we still know, in our hearts, it is unfair if the U.S., 4 percent of the world, contributes 25 percent of carbon emissions, more per person than any other country. Unfair for poor countries in Africa and the Pacific Islands, having done nothing to create global warming (90 percent caused by developed nations) to suffer floods and droughts, making agriculture and life impossible. For banks to get huge loans at taxpayers' expense, the banks making record profits, giving bonuses larger than the debt of many cities and more than the cost of health care for whole countries. For people to lose homes because they have lost work and gotten sick; for insurance companies, pharmaceuticals, banks, and energy corporations to prevent universal health care, competition for cheap drugs, banking regulation, and protection of water, air, and earth. Unfair that their millions of dollars are more powerful than the needs of millions. We all know what is fair, what is unfair.

We speak about freedom as if it is "I can do whatever I want whenever I want." Freedom as no restraint, no responsibility for consequences of our actions. We ignore the suffering of millions of people, call scientific research a hoax, scoff at years of dedicated labor to protect our earth for our grand-children. These are the words of a bully in the school yard asserting privilege based on power.

We know what is a fair wage, a fair profit, a fair cost. We know what is good for all living beings on this earth and for this earth.

Buddhists say that awareness is simple but not easy. For this holiday I wish us the peace and freedom that come from that simple awareness.

January 30th, 2010
Who will protect us from corporations?

The recent Supreme Court decision declared that because corporations are "persons" they have the First Amendment right of free speech. Translated, that means that corporations may spend unlimited amounts of their obscene profits to influence elections through media saturation and propaganda. The insurance and pharmaceutical companies and the financial and energy interests already spend millions on lobbying. Now with unlimited financial contributions, they will effectively select their candidates and write legislation.

In Ecuador's 2007 Constitution, nature is protected from corporations which, for decades, destroyed much of the Amazon forests, polluted waters, and poisoned people and animals. According to the indigenous concept of Sumac Kawsay "good living," "nature has the right to exist, maintain and regenerate its vital cycles, structure, functions, and its processes in evolution."

Whose rights do we recognize and protect?

In his "Beyond Vietnam," Martin Luther King Jr. spoke of our need for a "radical revolution of values," a shift from a "thing oriented society" where "machines and computers, profit motives and property rights are considered more important than people," to a "person-oriented society." King spoke of the good samaritan "on life's roadside," but went further: "One day we must come to see that the whole Jericho road must be transformed so that men and women will not be constantly beaten and robbed as they make their journey on life's highway. True compassion is more than flinging a coin to a beggar. It comes to see that an edifice which produces beggars needs restructuring."

To restructure and protect our democracy, we need public funding for elections so that those who govern are elected by and for the people, not chosen by and for profits of corporations. There is something terribly wrong with a country that protects rights of corporations above the rights of nature and "good living" of all beings.

December 3rd, 2011
Who is a "person,""what is a death panel," whose rights are protected, what is permitted, what is true "security"...and who has the power to "name"

Who is a "person?" Who has rights? Who is protected?

Corporations are "persons," their profits are protected. Corporate criminals are immune from punishment. Meanwhile 49,000,000 fall into poverty, the gap between rich and poor widens, workers' jobs and benefits are cut.

In Mississippi, people vote whether a fertilized egg is a "person." Meanwhile, U.S. infant mortality ranks 27th, childhood poverty increases, funding is cut for maternal care, food, education and protection of air and water.

Doctors informing patients of medical conditions and options are misnamed "a death panel." Palliative care, extending quality of life, is replaced with costly, unnecessary medical intervention prolonging suffering. The poverty of the elderly has increased sharply due to medical expenses, yet Congress seeks to cut Medicare and Social Security, two lifesaving programs.

Over 50 percent of federal taxes go to military for "security." Meanwhile we deny the greatest threat and danger to earth - catastrophic climate change.

Concealed guns are permitted in schools, legislatures, national parks, while marriage between loving people is prohibited.

In 1944, FDR proposed an "Economic Bill of Rights" declaring every human entitled to "earn enough to provide adequate food, clothing, recreation," to have a decent home, adequate medical care, a good education, to be protected "from economic fears of old age, sickness, accident and unemployment." Different townships, like Chambersburg, Pa., recognizing that "the political, legal, economic systems of the U.S. allow an elite few to impose policy and govern decisions that threaten the very survival of human and natural communities," declare their right "to revoke the authority of the corporate minority" and "codify new, sustainable systems."

The 99 percent/Occupy movement is part of an awakening to justice, declaring our rights as sovereign persons in a democracy. Not a fertilized egg, not a corporation, not the privileged few, but children, women, workers, the old, and our right to live in a living breathing earth.

January 7th, 2012
GOP adopts tea party and conservative dogma

It's strange hearing Republican candidates continually changing previous reasonable positions to step in line with tea party/Conservative dogma: denying evidence of climate change; retracting criticism of Ryan's plan to destroy Social Security and Medicare; denouncing beneficial medical reform; restricting women's choices.

The problem isn't changing one's mind if it's based on deepening awareness: former skinheads painfully removing racist and anti-Semitic tattoos that now repulse them; whistleblowers revealing and renouncing criminal actions of corporations and government; apartheid police feeling true remorse about harms they've committed; Lincoln writing the Emancipation Proclamation, recognizing abolition of slavery as the moral center of the Union cause. These are not "flip flops" but growing our souls.

The desert fathers defined "sin" as the refusal to grow. The opposite of sin then is the choice to grow, to look closely, to question, to make connections, to learn from experience. I'm inspired by those who walk this earth with eyes and heart open: Eleanor Roosevelt, Pete Seeger, Harry Belafonte… Grace Boggs, now 96, still struggles for radical social change in Detroit and around the world, always exploring different paths of transformation. Her long-time friend wrote, "Grace thinks, changes. She's constantly re-evaluating, open to new ideas." I think of Martin Luther King, Jr. whose "dream" kept expanding beyond race and color to an understanding of the deep connection between war, violence, racism, poverty. Speaking against the Vietnam War and for the garbage workers' strike, he demonstrated the incredible integrity and courage of a man whose heart and mind refused to stop learning and growing.

The question for all of us this new year and always is not whether we change our point of view, but the reason why, whether we choose to grow, to learn from experience, or contract in fear and expediency to our smaller selves.

February 21st, 2012
Greed is behind proposed pipeline

The proposed Keystone XL tar sands pipeline would transport 3.7 million gallons of extremely dirty coal (three times more carbon pollution) every day over 1,700 miles, across eight states, the Ogallah aquifer, thousands of streams and precious habitat, in pipes that already have leaked 14 times, recently spilling one million gallons of crude into the Kalamazoo River. Gingrich, to great laughter and applause, called President Obama's decision to investigate environmental effects "stupid." The Republicans push and threaten.

It is not for "jobs" (since there will be many fewer than proclaimed) or energy independence (since most oil will be shipped abroad, U.S. receiving equal amounts of crude from Canada whether or not the pipeline is built) It is the power of money.

Those 234 congressional representatives aggressively pushing for no review received $42,000,000 in campaign contributions from big oil.

Whether to destroy EPA's power to protect the environment, or consumer protection, health care reform, regulation of banks, those in power pay to protect their profits and privileges.

The U.S. Chamber of Commerce gave 94 percent of their enormous contributions to climate change deniers. The result - every GOP presidential candidate denies global climate change, a reality recognized by 97 percent of world scientists and experienced every day in intense hurricanes, droughts, floods and new illnesses.

On one side we have oil, gas, chemical companies and their millions spent on lobbying, PACS, and campaigns of disinformation. On the other, we have water, air, children, the old, scientists, doctors, researchers, and courageous people risking lives to protect earth, our only home. Who would you believe?

How did "they" get us to scoff at facts, believe that deregulation and lowering taxes on large corporations and millionaires would solve the very problems that unregulated capitalism created, to believe that nonrenewable dirty fossil fuels "cheap" and protecting earth "stupid?"

February 29th, 2012
GOP reinventing Reagan's bad ideas

Cultural amnesia and mass delusion are common. Republican candidates seem desperate to be Reaganites. But it was Reagan whose "trickle down economics," lowering taxes on the wealthy and corporations, plummeted us into debt, our economy restored only by the courage of President Bush Sr. who raised taxes and enraged the Republican Party. Rather than Reagan, we should look to FDR who brought our country out of depression, using government as ally, not enemy, creating jobs, building roads and infrastructures, providing safety nets, regulating the unbridled greed which almost destroyed us. In his 1937 inaugural address, FDR said, "We have always known that heedless self interest was bad morals; we know now that it is bad economics. We are beginning to abandon our tolerance of the abuse of power by those who betray for profit the elementary decencies of life. The test of progress is not whether we add more to the abundance of those who have much; it is whether we provide enough for those who have too little."

How different the dismal discourse now. Republican candidates rage against government and all regulations. They advocate bestowing more on those who have too much and taking from those who have too little, continually attempting to dismantle Social Security and Medicare. They have neither morality nor memory. It's good to remember the wisdom of an earlier Republican, President Eisenhower, who said in 1954, "Should any political party attempt to abolish Social Security, unemployment insurance, and eliminate labor laws, you would not hear of that party again in our political history. There is a tiny splinter group, of course, that believes you can do these things. Among them are Texas oil millionaires and an occasional politician or businessman. Their number is negligible and they are stupid."

Unfortunately their numbers have increased, some running for president.

May 3rd, 2012
On a personal note about our caring community

Since fire destroyed our home, we have experienced many acts of kindness. We want to acknowledge the goodness in people and express our gratitude for the generosity of friends and neighbors.

Neighbors quickly offered us places to stay and warm clothes and blankets, as well as words of sympathy. Even those who hardly knew us came by and offered help. Friends donated money, clothes, tools, music, flowers and books. Pure and Simple generously provided health food at no cost; the deBlasiis Concert series replenished our subscription tickets for their extraordinary concerts at the Hyde; folksingers Cindy Mangsen and Steve Gillette and Friends of Harmony gifted us with music CDs; Old Songs gave T-shirts. The list goes on and on. The volunteer firefighters worked for many hours to extinguish the fire.

We have been touched by all this support. It has warmed our hearts and provided comfort in a time of stress. We deeply appreciate this caring community.

Thank you all very much. We will do our best to "pass it forward."

July 7th, 2012
Humans unwilling to protect future

Every morning I survey the damage done during the night and early morning; the hummingbird feeders on the ground, the plastic yellow petals scattered and chewed; the metal feeder buried out of sight; the plastic feeder with large gaps requiring constant repair.

I say to the chipmunks, squirrels and raccoons: "There is enough for everyone; you're destroying your food source, your future sustenance." I say, "Look beyond your nose and mouth." But they cannot. They take more than their share. They continue to do what is harmful to themselves and the living community.

How could I not think of us, the human animal, and our strange inability to see the effects of our action: we want what we want when we want it. How to explain our poisoning of air, water and earth — our sustenance; our willingness to dump sewage in rivers, poisons in food, mercury in air; our not seeing connections between environmental abuse and childhood development, asthma, chronic heart diseases, cancers.

And how, with vivid pictures of devastation — fire storms, floods, intense heat, 10-year droughts, water tables lowering, snow packs diminishing — can we deny climate change and our addiction to the nonrenewable fossil fuels whose greenhouse gasses threaten our living earth?

I hear the scoffing at science, the chanting of "drill baby drill," the push to dismantle the clean air and clean water regulations, the not remembering oil spills, nuclear disasters, undrinkable water, toxic chemicals.

I wonder at our capacity of denial, at how our minds, which could and should be able to see more than chipmunks and squirrels, could be so misled by those who deceive for profits, who continually take more than their share. How could we be so separate from our bodies and the Earth to sell our birthright, destroy our source of life?

August 20th, 2012
Politicians need to re-examine moral values

A disclaimer: I'm on Social Security and Medicare. I love national and state parks, concerts in Lake George, films, music and art at Crandall Public Library. I'm nourished by public television and radio, their science, history, culture and news. I am deeply committed to public education, public transportation and medical care (providing preventative treatment, excluding no one for pre-existing conditions, being affordable for all). I am thankful our government helps communities suffering from hurricanes, tornadoes, droughts. I want clean air and water, diversity of plants and animals. And I'm very disturbed that some, in the name of fiscal responsibility, would destroy what enriches our communities and our lives.

Ayn Rand, Ryan's philosophical hero, values selfishness, greed, competition and individualism and dismisses kindness, empathy, compassion, community. Not only are these new breed Republicans morally bereft, they are economically ignorant.

Reducing even further the already low taxes on the wealthy and huge corporations has not and will not create jobs. It will make the already wealthy richer, increase deficits, increase taxes on working people and devastate services.

The work program of FDR, their "enemy," brought millions back to work and ended the depression brought on by his Republican predecessor. He said and I believe: "We have always known that heedless self-interest was bad morals; we know now that it is bad economics. Out of the collapse of a prosperity whose builders boasted their practicality has come the conviction that, in the long run, economic morality pays."

Had some Republicans, in their hard-hearted greed and ideological rigidity, not blocked every job creation program, Obama might have had similar success.

The 1 percent can buy an election, disenfranchise legal voters, and bombard us with lies and propaganda, convincing us to vote against our real interests and deeper morality. The question is what kind of world do we want to live in?

October 6th, 2012
Better wages would boost our economy

Last week, I paid $50 for gas. Sneakers cost $25. My friend couldn't afford a dentist. I thought of the federal minimum wage, $7.25 an hour, and the four million Americans paid at or below that; wondered how they live, eat, pay rent and utilities, raise children, get gas or fix their car, teeth or body. How they nourish body and spirit.

Those voting against raising the minimum wage claimed most minimum wage workers are young, working part time. The reality: 6.4 percent are teenagers, the rest adults, many single mothers. Romney's statement that 47 percent didn't pay federal income tax ignored their paying payroll, state, local and sales taxes, and the reality that struggling workers and those on Social Security earned too little to pay federal income tax. I thought of CEOs earning 450 times what average workers earn and the big recipients of government "welfare" handouts: oil, gas, coal, agribusiness, global corporations, banks.

We all have a sense of what's right: we want to punish criminals, stop corruption, have good work, receive a fair wage. No one should earn less than needed to survive; no one earn so much they can buy elections.

There's one simple way to increase the amount paid into federal income taxes, reduce our deficit, and get work for the unemployed. Return to the past progressive tax structure and pay a liveable wage, at least $10 an hour. When people earn more, they buy; the economy is stimulated, businesses flourish, workers are hired. As a country, we'd return the promise of the American Dream.

We work to earn money to live, but it's more — pride in the work of our hands, hearts and mind, a sense of worth, of dignity. A hundred years ago women strikers in Lowell marched for higher wages. Their song, "Give us bread, but give us roses." Yes, "bread and roses."

October 21st, 2012
Earth must be taken care of; it is our only home

Our Earth has been strangely absent from political debates, as if we didn't breathe air, drink water, get nourished by food, as if we were not totally dependent on her for life.

At the Republican Convention, Romney scoffed at Obama's speaking of water rising, as if global warming and climate change weren't real — the intensity of devastating storms, flooding, droughts, record heat and melting ice.

Instead of competing for allowing more drilling everywhere, I wanted someone to speak about the fragility of Earth, the importance of EPA's regulating mercury and toxins, protecting our air and water, and the high cost of seeming low cost energy — the grave dangers of dirty coal, drilling in the Arctic, of fracking and the tar sands pipeline. Instead they speak of the illusion of "good jobs," most of which come from out of state, are short lived and leave environmental devastation in their wake.

Energy independence and jobs don't come from increasing dependence on fossil fuels but on renewable energy, job retraining, building infrastructures and conserving. I understand why oil, gas and coal pay millions to lobby and lie: to continue profit and privilege. What's painful is to hear us cheer them and condemn those fighting to preserve our only home.

Romney has already told us his first acts if elected: to approve the XL Keystone pipeline, remove environmental protections, appeal Obama's affordable health care, and defund public television, Planned Parenthood and Head Start. He would protect the rights of corporations from regulations and limit women's health rights.

I want leaders to protect the rights of Earth, of communities to determine what happens to their water and air, of women to determine what happens to their bodies, of children (both born and unborn) to inherit a healthy living Earth, rich in diversity, bounty and beauty.

That, it seems to me, is most deeply pro-life.

June 18th, 2013
Whistleblowers are courageous people: what is legal and what is illegal

If it were April Fool's Day, I could believe what seems absurd. We "legally" prevent disclosure of huge donors to political PACs; dangerous chemicals in household products; GMOs in food; poisons used in fracking. It's illegal to take photos of animal abuse in factory farms and reveal deep corruption in corporations, banks and government; it's considered "espionage" to bring to light wide surveillance by private corporations hired by NSA, expose illegal and problematic acts of military or government, or make public our "Free Trade" agreements that hurt our workers, undermine subsistence economies and empower corporations to sue for unmade "future profits" if a country (or city or state) sues them for polluting their environment and causing illness. Equally absurd and immoral is that in our country, with its increasing gap between the wealthy and the poor and with hunger on the rise, the Republicans cut food stamps, double interest on student loans, and reduce funding for Head Start and public education.

Perhaps most strange is how, despite evidence — glaciers melting, severe drought, record heat, floods, intense storms — a large number of Republicans still doubt what 98 percent of scientists confirm, still subsidize fossil fuels, promote the XL Keystone pipeline, cut moneys for renewable energy, and seek to weaken the clean air and water acts.

Throughout history there are those who, for personal power or profit, do grave harm to many. And there are those whose courage and personal integrity compel them to work for the common good, exposing dangers to air and water; creating national parks; working for animal and human rights, fair wages and safe working conditions; and, most recently, risking imprisonment and life by exposing threats by our government to our democracy.

I think of Bradley Manning, Edward Snowden and whistleblowers throughout history exposing what those in power wish to silence. I thank them for their courage.

September 30th, 2013
Who are all these people doing this?

My bumper sticker reads: "Never have so few taken so much from so many for so long." Of all developed countries, the U.S. has the largest (and increasing) gap between wealthy and poor, the highest infant mortality, the greatest percentage of incarcerated people. Productivity has increased, but the median wage has gone down. People are losing homes, food pantries are depleted. Yet, unbelievably, there are some who vote against increasing the minimum wage, who vote to cut food stamps and Medicaid, who would privatize Medicare and Social Security, who would defund Head Start, close women's clinics, stop job training programs and subsidies for renewable energy.

Who are these anti-life people who fight any regulation protecting consumers, workers, air, water and who deny what science and experience make very clear: the terrible cost of global warming (the intensity and frequency of fires, drought, heat, floods) caused by our addiction to fossil fuels?

Like all tyrants, they hold hostages until their demands are met — for the Keystone XL Pipeline and for a delay in the Affordable Care laws. As the cigarette companies declared cigarettes safe and chemical companies swore DDT was harmless, corporations lie, using money from corporate sponsors to spread propaganda. Tar sands oil is not safe, has already destroyed streams and aquifers; the oil would be shipped abroad, not making us energy independent, and the pipeline won't create local jobs but endanger water and air. And Obamacare would allow people choice in an open free market, competition reducing premiums and the federal government granting tax credit to businesses and financial aide to individuals.

Who are these anti-life people lacking both compassion and understanding? Who would destroy our economy and county and, for greed, sacrifice the diversity and beauty of our living earth?

December 2nd, 2013
Our choices could help environment

How close does something have to be to see "it," to recognize cause and effect, to choose wisely? How many intense tornadoes, hurricanes, floods, droughts, fires? How much unbreathable air, toxic water, oil leaks and pipe disasters? How many lakes once teeming with fish now depleted? How many birds and pollinating bees gone? How much beauty and diversity lost?

How much objective scientific research is needed to understand connections between fossil fuels, climate change and world suffering — famines, refugees fleeing, wars?

People disagree. But if we look closely at our experience of well-being and what gives us joy, if we look at our children and grandchildren and their future, if we love beauty (mountains, flowers, trees, coral reefs, animals), I think we know what is most precious and must be preserved. How did we get so far from this knowing, so disconnected from our Earth, our only home?

Fossil fuels are not "cheap" energy: they're costly. Look around. I think of those whose greed is insatiable, whose money enables them to buy politicians and convince us, through media propaganda, to "choose" paths of destruction. Who should we believe? Coal, oil, gas corporations or 98 percent of world scientists, those who struggle to protect water, air, Earth and our own deeper wisdom?

It's important to redefine: Who are the criminals and who the heroes?

What is justice? What is fair? Who profits and who suffers? We can't change natural laws, but through awareness, we can recognize the disastrous effects of our actions. We can cap emissions, charge carbon taxes, conserve energy, and make real investments in renewable resources, giving us both the jobs we want and an environment we need.

Awareness is revolutionary, especially if tied to action and change. It enables us to actually choose, to choose life over death.

April 10th, 2014
Save your rage for that which destroys

Alabama unanimously outlawed sustainability and any plan traced to the United Nations' Agenda 21, a nonbinding voluntary plan for global sustainability signed by George H.W. Bush.

Championed by the Republican National Committee, the law bans funding for organizations that help implement Agenda 21: Wetlands Watch, city planners, environmental consultants. I thought it was an April Fool's joke.

I think about what's illegal: labeling genetically modified food, disclosing chemicals involved in fracking, taking photographs of animal cruelty at factory farms. Animal and environmental whistleblowers are charged as terrorists.

A lot defies reason: Governors in poor states with hospitals closing and thousands uninsured are refusing the federal government's expansion of fully funded Medicaid; Congress is cutting food stamps and rejecting increases in minimum wage; there is venomous hatred toward Obamacare, which expands insurance to those with pre-existing conditions, increases the number of insured, closes the doughnut hole and provides free preventive care.

There's much one could and should be enraged about: incredible income inequality; attacks on workers and unions; outsourcing of jobs; restrictions on voter registration; closing women's health clinics; the terrible "cost" of "cheap" fossil fuels; floods, hurricanes and continual spills and accidents poisoning our streams, rivers, drinking water, wildlife and health.

It's painful to hear people cheering those who would harm them and cursing those who protect. Goebbels, Hitler's propaganda minister, spoke of propaganda's power to make people believe "a square is a circle," sustainability is communism, privatizing schools and Social Security is freedom, global climate change is a hoax. Big money buys politicians and media. Lies coated with fears continually bombard us.

The antidote to propaganda is clear and careful thought, reality checks and questioning vested interests. It's looking closely at one's own experiences and what really creates a healthy, vibrant community. How could one not want to sustain and conserve life?

July 12th, 2014
Time to redefine 'pro-life,' 'freedom'

The Founding Fathers knew the power of religion to divide people. To protect both religion and country, they created a wall of separation between the two, the First Amendment stating: "Congress shall make no law respecting an establishment of religion or prohibiting the free exercise thereof." George Washington consciously removed all mention of Christianity in public documents.

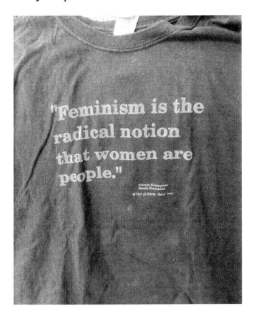

Looking around the world, we can see their prophetic wisdom; the grave danger of any religion arrogantly assuming it's the "truth" and attempting to impose that truth on others, especially on women. In the recent Supreme Court decision, five Catholic men under the guise of "religious freedom" and the legal absurdity that "corporations are persons," allowed private corporations their "religious freedom" to impose their will on female workers, denying them free contraception under Obamacare.

I had a bumper sticker: "Feminism is the radical notion that a woman is a person." In poor countries, there's direct correlation between women's access to birth control and their family and country's economic health and well-being. Yet patriarchal religious institutions there and here continually attempt control over women by defining contraception as sinful.

We need to redefine "pro-life" as the rights of women to control their bodies, the rights of all to free medical care, good public education, meaningful jobs, livable wages. And we need to redefine "freedom" as the rights of communities to say "no" to corporations that poison air, water, earth, destroy neighborhoods and farms, make sterile the bounty and beauty of this Earth for their profit and control.

August 29th, 2014
Vote for candidates who speak for you

As long as politicians need enormous amounts of money to win elections, each party will court big money and be beholden to their wishes. The vast majority of Americans were against Bush/Cheney's invasion of Iraq, yet Congress — Democrats and Republicans — supported this illegal, unwise war that unleashed disastrous consequences now visible in sectarian violence. Both parties support free trade (not fair trade), hurting American workers, destroying subsistence economies abroad and protecting profits of huge corporations over environmental protection and workers' rights.

Without campaign finance reform, both parties will be ruled by powerful moneyed interests creating a plutocracy rather than democracy. But still there are choices in every election, real differences. It's almost inconceivable women would vote for a party that consistently votes against equal pay for equal work, against women's reproductive rights, against protection of women from violence. Or that workers would vote for a party that votes against raising the minimum wage and has, from Reagan on, done everything to destroy workers' rights to organize; that older Americans would vote for a party that would privatize Social Security and Medicare; that anyone who drinks water and breathes air wouldn't want them protected; that everyone wouldn't want to close tax loopholes, penalize corporations that outsource, and reward corporations and small businesses that create jobs at home; that we all wouldn't see that it is not the trickle down taxes for the wealthy but people working, earning and spending money that creates a healthy, sustainable economy.

Sen. James Jeffords, a conservative Republican from Vermont, recently died. He left the Republican Party because he felt it left him, betrayed what he most valued — education, environment, fairness and justice. We need to reform the whole system of elections. In the meantime, we have to vote for those who give voice to what we most value.

October 21st, 2014
Republican history precludes Stefanik

Gerda Lerner's "Why History Matters" speaks of the importance of remembering personal and world history to learn from the past. And I think of our history: How FDR brought us out of the Depression by increasing government spending, the WPA and CCC creating jobs, building roads and infrastructure, invigorating our economy and spirit. I think of Reagan's "trickle down economics," cutting taxes on the wealthy, undercutting workers, driving our country into debt. And i think how Clinton balanced our budget, raising taxes and refusing to privatize Social Security and Medicare despite Gingrich and Republicans closing down the government to impose their will.

I think how history can be distorted, how Republicans used Swift Boat lies making Kerry, who received Bronze and Silver Star Medals and Purple Hearts, seem dishonorable, and how now Obama is attacked for causing ISIS, the seeds of which were planted by Bush/Cheney's disastrous unprovoked costly war in Iraq. Goebbels, the Naza propagandist, wrote: "It would not be impossible to prove with sufficient repetition that a square is in fact a circle."

The Republican platform seems empty, their main goal attacking Obama on everything, making his Affordable Care Act, increasing coverage for millions, the "enemy" and offering no alternative. They advocate decreasing taxes on the wealthy, cutting food stamps, defunding subsidies for renewable energies, increasing subsidies to fossil fuels, blocking citizens from voting and women from health care, defunding Planned Parenthood, voting against pay equity and increasing the minimum wage, blocking refinancing of student loans and blocking immigration reform. What is their real program?

Stefanik speaks of being bipartisan, but look at the Republican platform, which she helped write. Look closely at policies, at actions. Think what really creates a healthy economy and healthy world.

November 2nd, 2014
Money can sway democratic process

I too am fearful of the power of big money, big corporations, and secret big PACS to shape our policies, our government, and our own minds and hearts, how they "advertise" their products and their candidates to sell us what we don't want or need, how they endanger democracy.

We all need good work with fair wages, shelter, food, medical care — need to survive. But when we suffer loss (of home, loved ones, health) we also realize what else is really important — kindness, caring, family, community, beauty, a clear stream, clean water and air. We have been taught to believe progress is growth rather than sustainability, success means earning enormous wealth, and that our Earth and our bodies are commodities, not living beings. We have lost touch with what is most precious.

I see the Republican platform as anti-life. Their main campaign tactic is to viciously attack Obamacare, which has helped millions to health care, as if it's evil, and to blame him for everything: Ebola, ISIS, immigrants. Meanwhile, they vote against raising minimum wage, pay equity for women, subsidizing sustainable energies, removing subsidies for companies that outsource. They would even give more tax breaks to those who have too much and take from those struggling just to live. And they restrict voting wherever they can, limiting accessibility and claiming nonexistent voter fraud to demand voter identification, allowing licenses for concealed weapons but not student IDs. Their tactics are transparent –as is their closing women's health care facilities "to protect women's health."

There are thoughtful moderate Republicans dismayed at the hardhearted rigid ideology of their own party. Stefanik is not one of them. She helped write the Republican platform. I see Aaron Woolf, running on the Working Families and Democratic line, as someone thoughtful and fair, concerned about workers, women, families, small farms and businesses, and working to create healthy caring communities.

November 14th, 2014
Greed won in the midterm elections

It's clear who won big this election: big money, big corporations, fossil fuels, Monsanto. And who lost: the Earth and all its inhabitants. McConnell, new majority speaker, has pledged to "compromise" — Keystone XL Pipeline, fracking, drilling. With Obama, they would support fast-tracking the Trans-Pacific trade agreement, the secretive corporate deal allowing private companies to sue for any environmental, health or worker regulations limiting their present or future profits. The "Buy America" provision allowing government contracts to favor our workers and companies would be a "violation," facilitating agreements going to the lowest international bidder. There will be amnesty, not for immigrants but for corporations who have paid no taxes for years. The $4 billion spent on this election will reap rewards: reducing regulations on clean air and water and coal emissions, reducing funds for EPA and national parks, defunding scientific innovative research creating jobs for a sustainable Earth. Inhofe, a climate change denier, will head the Senate Environmental Committee. For a powerful country to support ignorance is more than embarrassing, it is shameful and dangerous.

There were bright lights: voters approved increasing the minimum wage; Chevron, spending millions to load the City Council in Richmond, California, lost; the anti-GMO initiative won in Maui despite the millions spent by Monsanto to misinform. The "right to know" movement is spreading — right to know what's in our foods, in fracking chemicals, in trade deals — as is the movement of communities saying "we the people," not the corporations, have a right to determine what happens to our land, Earth, children.

I feel deep gratitude to those past and present who, with integrity and courage, struggle to protect our common good against the forces of greed and power, who recognize the great web that connects all beings and act to preserve life on planet Earth, our only home.

January 24th, 2015
Words reverberated in other speeches

   Reading Dr. King's words, I wonder if those who now praise him, especially those in power, have actually read anything other than his 1963 powerful "I have a dream speech" in Washington, D.C., if they followed his journey of mind, heart and spirit through the next four years to his "Beyond Vietnam" speech on April 4, 1967, in Riverside Church, to his support of sanitation workers in Memphis and to his plans for a poor people's tent city in the capital.

   I think how we romanticize our "heroes," ignoring truths they risk their lives to speak. In 1967, King spoke of the need for "a radical revolution of values," a "shift from a thing-oriented" society to a "person-oriented society," warning that when "profit motives and property rights are considered more important than people, the giant triplets of racism, materialism and militarism are incapable of being conquered," declaring that "true compassion is more than flinging a coin to a beggar," and that "an edifice which produces beggars needs restructuring" and a country "that spends more on military defense than on programs of social uplift is approaching spiritual death."

   King was a prophet understanding cause and effect and warning us of the grave dangers of our actions. I'm inspired by his nonviolence, love, wisdom and his ability to articulate so clearly issues of his time, of our time. Like all whistleblowers whose "conscience leaves no choice," King was condemned by those in power, even his own black community, for going beyond "a dream" to an understanding of the connection between violence, poverty and racism. May we who praise him actually hear his prophetic words: "Our only hope today lies in our ability to recapture the revolutionary spirit and go out into a sometimes hostile world declaring eternal hostility to poverty, racism and militarism."

March 20th, 2015
GOP is angry at all the wrong things

There's much to be angry at: Corporate takeover of our country, moneyed interests buying elections through media propaganda, extreme income inequality, poisoning air, water and earth, causing increases in cancer, autism and Alzheimer's; loss of species and diversity; and flooding, droughts and intense storms. But instead of getting to the root causes, we rage against false enemies.

Many Republicans still deny human contribution to global climate change, pushing for drilling everywhere, removing protection of air and water, withdrawing subsidies for renewable energy with its economic and sustainable promise. (Florida's governor silenced governmental agencies from mentioning "global climate change," his state most vulnerable to rising waters of glacial melt.)

The main "policy" of McConnell and many Republicans is attack: Impeach President Barack Obama for immigration reform while refusing debate on immigration; repeal Obamacare offering no alternative; vote against increasing minimum wage, funds for infrastructure and education; and refuse to change any of their outrageous tax breaks for the wealthy.

They have brought up Benghazi for eight different investigations and now rant about Hillary Clinton's emails. Their "vision" for America: drill, undercut workers and unions, remove regulation of banks, Wall Street and polluters, send ground troops, and condemn diplomacy as "weakness." They attempt to undercut John Kerry, Obama and the multinational attempt at diplomacy with Iran, their action, viewed by many moderate Republicans, as unprecedented and outrageous.

Other than attacking, what do they actually believe?

August 26th, 2015
Pro-birth, pro-life are very different

Sister Joan Chittister, a Catholic nun, redefines "pro-life": "I do not believe that just because you're opposed to abortion that makes you pro-life. In fact, I think in many cases your morality is deeply lacking if all you want is a child born, but not a child fed, not a child educated, not a child housed. Why would I think that? Because you don't want any tax money to go there. That's not pro-life. That's pro-birth. We need a much broader conversation on what the morality of pro-life is."

As part of that conversation, I offer my thoughts on pro-life: Respecting all life, recognizing our connection and interdependence. Increasing, not privatizing Social Security, easily made solvent by removing the $125,000 cap for payments. Expanding Medicare to include eyes, ears, teeth, saving money through competitive bidding for pharmaceuticals, now outlawed. Promoting voting rights, not blocking by claiming (nonexistent) voter fraud. Supporting worldwide programs promoting women's reproductive health and choices (and helping control unsustainable population growth), Planned Parenthood, contraception, sex education. Supporting increases in minimum wages and retraining those needing new skills. Supporting, not defunding and selling to the highest bidders our common lands — parks, forests, wilderness where we walk, swim, hike and fish.

Pope Frances' encyclical "On the Care of Our Common Home" speaks of man-made climate change "as a global problem with grave implications," of economic policies contributing to poverty and the "unprecedented destruction of ecosystems." He says, "Every effort to protect and improve our world entails profound changes in lifestyles, models of production and consumption, and the established structures of power which today govern societies." He and I "beg the Lord to grant us more politicians who are genuinely disturbed by the state of society, the people, the lives of the poor," who are truly pro-life.

November 5th, 2015
Let's keep fighting for a better world

    This morning I heard students speak about Upward Bound, how it enabled them to succeed in high school and prepare for college. At night, I went to a folk concert at Crandall, partially funded by New York State Council on the Arts. Every month I receive Social Security and Medicare, not entitlements, but rather programs I paid into for 30 years. Last May I camped in Zion and Bryce, two of many incredible national parks. And here, where I live, bike paths, nature trails, free concerts. I feel deeply appreciative of programs by the federal, state and local governments that enrich me and our community.

    It is not "austerity" and trickle-down economics that make a country "wealthy"; they impoverish both spirit and economy. People need to feel a sense of worth and possibility. Under FDR, the Civilian Conservation Corps, the Public Works Program and the WPA gave people meaningful jobs in reforestation, conservation, infrastructure, construction, arts and theater. The National Labor Relations Board established codes of fair competition, minimum wages and collective bargaining. Under Johnson's "war on poverty" we had Medicaid, Medicare, food stamps, Head Start, Job Corps, VISTA and Title 1. We had a civil rights and voting rights act.

    I think of the backlash to goodness, about our movement backwards: to limit voting access and to gerrymander; to privatize Social Security, schools, prisons, water; to limit Medicaid, restrict collective bargaining, defund community programs, restrict research on the effects of gun violence or environmental poisoning; to sue a community's ability to label GMOs and ban fracking or plastics.

    This Thanksgiving I give thanks to those who, throughout history, have struggled for a better and more just world, who fought and fight to preserve the common good: workers, African Americans, women, immigrants, gays, teachers, musicians, firemen, nurses, whistleblowers, environmentalists ... the list is long.

December 1st, 2015
Hate makes us be terrorists we hate

Thank you Will Doolittle for your "Let's Welcome Refugees" asking us to think rather than react in rage against wrong "enemies." No Syrians were involved in the Paris attacks. Hijackers involved in Sept. 11 were mainly Saudis, "friends" we spend billions rearming who commit human rights abuses, are bombing civilians in Yemen, are the home to Wahhabism, a radical Sunni fundamentalism. Before 9/11, we supported bin Laden and terrorists in Afghanistan fighting against Russia. After 9/11, we invaded Iraq, not our "enemy," for nonexistent "weapons of mass destruction," our actions causing unintended consequences in Iraq, Syria, Afghanistan, millions of refugees now seeking a safe home. Europe has opened its doors to hundreds of thousands of Syrian refugees, Canada will admit 25,000. We have taken in only 2,000. Now many politicians and governors want to close all doors to Syrian refugees.

I too am afraid of acts of terrorism by ISIS, but afraid also of all terrorism to all beings and to our earth. I am very afraid of hate that fuels violence. Aldous Huxley wrote about "herd poisoning," how through propaganda, people are herded into acts of unthinkable violence against "the other," whether in Nazi Germany or Rwanda or here. I am frightened when I hear a governor justify closing our borders using the example of our disgraceful internment of Japanese American citizens during World War II

and when a presidential candidate justifies waterboarding and torture to thunderous cheers. Ben Franklin said, "He who would trade liberty for some temporary security deserves neither liberty nor security." In fear and rage we become the terrorists we hate.

We destroy friends by making them enemies, casting them out, dehumanizing them. One way to defeat "enemies" is to make them our friends, welcoming, as the Bible says, the stranger who was ourselves.

58

February 4th, 2016
We have the power to make life better

There is much to fear, but being killed by Syrian refugee families fleeing from violence is not one of them. More frightening are the omnipresent poisons in our environment — pesticides, fertilizers, processed foods–all disrupting hormones and causing increases in asthma, cancers, diabetes, autism, Alzheimer's, birth defects. I'm more afraid of methane and oil leaking from pipes, lead poisoning and chemicals in water. If I were black, I'd be more afraid of white policemen; as a Muslim, more afraid of mosques being arsoned; as a woman, more afraid of sexual harassment, domestic violence, of Planned Parenthood and maternity hospitals being closed down, of contraception not covered by insurance because someone's "religious freedom" allows discrimination. As a worker, I'd fear jobs going overseas, corporations seeking cheap labor, corporate tax shelters and avoidance of environmental laws. I'm afraid of corporations ruling our world, the World Trade Organization's "free trade" allowing them to sue for loss of profit because of laws which require labeling, declaring the origin for meat, the banning of plastic or toxins, the stopping tar sands. I'm afraid for democracy, afraid of money buying elections, limiting voting rights, privatizing common land and resources. And I'm afraid for Earth — our addiction to fossil fuels causing catastrophic climate change, droughts, record heat, intense storms, climate refugees, wars over resources.

We're vulnerable; we'll die. The question is how we want to live, the illusion of safety preventing us from choosing what promotes life. We could hire workers to rebuild crumbling infrastructure, have more teachers, nurses, community health clinics; increase our minimum wage; have paid family leave. Corporations could pay for emissions and for the damages caused by those emissions; drug companies could pay for harm done by their products.; the prices for drugs could be negotiated. And the wealthy could pay a fair share of taxes.

Our schools have a "kindness curriculum." May our politicians learn that curriculum. Instead of bullying and building walls of hate, we could promote empathy and understanding, cooperation and dialogue. With wisdom we could work for equality and justice.

June 29th, 2016
Terrorism is woven into our society

We're horrified by acts of terrorism: Orlando, Charleston, San Bernardino, Newtown, Oklahoma City. What we see less clearly is the terrorism so interwoven in a culture it seems normal: colonialism, imperialism, slavery. It's terrorism against women by their intimate partners — three women killed every day, 4,774,000 women experiencing extreme violence every year. American troops killed in Afghanistan and Iraq between 2001 and 2012 numbered 6,488– during that same time 11,766 American women were murdered by current or former male partners.

I think of other homegrown unrecognized "terrorism": our violence toward Earth, our only home. Chemical and oil spills, methane leaks, toxic waste dumped into rivers, loss of coral reefs and wetlands, the ocean used as a garbage dump. Our Defense Department declared man-made climate change our greatest terrorist threat — depletion of water causing water wars, droughts and floods destroying crops and homes, millions of refugees fleeing violence and hunger. Here record heat, intensity of storms, wildfires, floods, yet the extraordinary denial of this "terrorism" and its root causes.

Terrorism as not just violence but an attitude toward others: viewing women, the Earth and other beings as objects to be used, abused, exploited, a feeling of separation and superiority allowing us to justify greed, power, privilege and cruelty.

Throughout history demagogues have manipulated people's fear, insecurity and anger, blaming "another" for all problems. In Nazi Germany Jews were easy scapegoats. Here it's Muslims, blacks, refugees, Mexicans, women, gays, abortion doctors. Rather than real institutional changes to create economic and racial justice, these "leaders" offer the illusion of security and promise of power by denigrating a chosen enemy. Dialogue, compromise, peace, empathy, friendship are seen as weakness. Concealed guns, military-style assault weapons, waterboarding, barrel bombing and rage are seen as manly strength.

And the question: what really makes us safe from terrorism against us and within us?

July 21st, 2016
Populism speaks to need for social justice

Watching PBS' centennial celebration of our national parks, I was moved by the incredible beauty of our country, grateful to those who protected and preserved places through the years for all of us.

What moved me was FDR's actions during the depression, employing the government to create jobs and alleviate suffering — CCC, WPA, farm programs, unemployment insurance. Workers built parks, roads, infrastructure, earning income and feeling pride in good work. Isn't that what demoralized, insecure, angry people need? Isn't that what Bernie touched in people — justified anger against growing inequality, corporate greed, Congress catering to the powerful, and the hope of economic security and justice? Perhaps that explains why some supported Trump.

But there's vast difference between the "populism" of Bernie and Trump.

Populism speaks to our desire for social justice for all. Building a wall is not building jobs. Denigrating unions, black lives matter, women, Muslims, Mexicans is not elevating human beings. Trump's exploiting workers, not paying taxes, abusing bankruptcy laws demonstrates arrogance and greed.

Bernie was a true populist. His struggle for democracy and justice for all pushed the Democratic Party to its better self. Their platform: protects and expands Social Security; moves toward a $15 minimum wage; closes loopholes allowing corporations to avoid paying taxes; enacts action to regulate banks and the greed of pharmaceutical companies; creates millions of jobs in infrastructure and green energy. The Republican platform: a wall between the U.S. and Mexico; repealing Obamacare, Dodd Frank reform, marriage equality; lowering corporate taxes and not taxing returned earnings from overseas; restricting women's access to health care; denying human caused climate change.

Anger can be fuel in the struggle for social injustice, but without reflection and understanding, it becomes unthinking rage, terrorism against innocent "enemies." Humans are capable of a range of behaviors — cruelty, greed, hatred but also generosity, kindness, wisdom. The question: which leaders inspire cooperation and justice and promote common goodness?

August 9th, 2016
Hatred is no way to debate issues

To counteract the harm of bullying, our schools cultivate empathy, putting oneself in another's shoes. Trump has mimicked the disabled, demeaned Mexicans, insulted women, spoke of shooting and punching people. Were Trump in my class, I'd report his dangerous behavior. Since the Trump campaign, bullying has increased; we imitate what we see and hear in schools, families, neighborhoods. The unifying theme at RNC was not an economic plan but demonization of Hillary, a chorus screaming "liar," "jail her," "kill her." As a possible president, Trump is terrifying – his arrogance, inexperience, ignorance and contempt.

Thoughtful debate over issues is essential for democracy, but hatred is impervious to reason, a death wish for the "chosen" cast out group. The Nazis knew if one keeps repeating a lie, people will believe it. For years Trump questioned Obama's citizenship and religion. For 25 years the Republicans have attacked Hillary – for fraud, conspiracy, Benghazi, emails – spending millions on investigations and trials but never proving any illegal behavior. I've disagreements with Hillary's hawkish foreign policy but immense respect for her continued hard work for children, families, health and justice. But with hate – misogyny, racism – it doesn't matter what someone says or does. Democracy demands discussion over real issues, not bullies threatening violence.

I loved the incredible diversity of age, class, type, color at the Democratic Convention, an inclusiveness welcoming all. In nature, diversity, interconnection and interdependence are the life force. What I see within the Republican party is a monoculture, a rigid authority with bullies threatening and wanting total control.

I hope Hillary does what she promises – economic, racial, gender justice, and water and earth rights. I fear Trump will do what he promises: a Putin-like violence, building walls, denigrating others, bankrupting our economy and democracy. I will work hard for my hope, the alternative too dangerous.

"If you see something, say something."

October 1st, 2016
Mike Derrick listens and aims to do good

 How close must something be before we see danger: Our child poisoned by lead in water, suffering asthma because of pollution; friends dying from cancers caused by toxins; lakes, rivers, and oceans contaminated by oil spills; record heat, intense storms, droughts, floods; local effects of climate change for farmers, snowless winters for our North Country. The question isn't whether we "believe" in global warming and its man-made causes, but why we deny what 98 percent of scientists, every nation in the world and our own experience recognize as reality, as true.

It's dangerous to have a presidential candidate declaring climate change a hoax, saying on his first day he'd abrogate commitments made in Paris and remove EPA regulations restricting toxic emissions. And it's incomprehensible to have climate change denial a central tenet of the Republican Party, their bills blocking clean air and water protections, defunding the EPA and national parks, handing our federally controlled public lands to mining and development interests.

In the past, conservation legislation had bipartisan support. Now compromise is blasphemy, defunding Planned Parenthood (based on falsified videos) a religious battle, restriction on voting rights a righteous campaign against nonexistent fraud. How could a party justify blocking Wall Street reforms and ethics' regulations? Vote against equal pay for equal work and raising minimum wage? For decreasing taxes for the already too wealthy? How not see green energy as the rapidly growing path to jobs for retrained workers and earth as our only home?

Elise Stefanik may be a good person, but she's been groomed to strictly adhere to a party that has ceased to support workers, women, earth and common good. In Mike Derrick, I see not an ideologue beholden to special interests but someone who listens closely, seeks fairness and understands the great potential within us and our region.

October 20th, 2016
Our sins are hurting our planet every day

On Yom Kippur, Jews reflect on how we've "missed the mark" and how, through awareness, we can choose to change, to grow. We recite the "alphabet of sins" — arrogance, bigotry, greed, hatred, xenophobia, zeal for wrong causes. We quote the prophets about feeding the hungry, welcoming the stranger, kindness, compassion, forgiveness, peace.

We confess our "sins" against the earth, assaulting our planet in countless ways; driving myriad species to extinction; exhausting irreplaceable resources; harming beyond repair habitats of living beings; jeopardizing well-being of future generations; questioning solid evidence of danger; spewing poisons into the bloodstream of land, rivers, lakes; losing sight of our role as God's partner in creation; using shared resources for personal gain and corporate profit; transforming dazzling beauty into industrial ugliness.

Our Defense Department calls climate change the greatest terrorist threat — floods, drought, desertification, fires, water wars, climate refugees. Warming waters and rising oceans increase intensity of storms, yet Trump would abrogate climate treaties, and Pence speaks about our "war on coal," repeating myths of "clean coal." The Republican platform denies man-made causes of global warming, as do Republican governors of states seeking federal help from climate devastation. Republicans have lost bipartisan care for earth. Their "religious" politics have narrowed "morality" to defunding Planned Parenthood. Stefanik votes her party's position.

James Baldwin writes of those who don't see and don't wish to see. Exxon Mobil did "see" in the '80s catastrophic effects of fossil fuels but spent and still spend millions suppressing what they know, funding candidates like Stefanik, who supports drilling and fossil fuel subsidies, and who vetoes regulations protecting air, water, health.

Ignorance isn't bliss. Emma Goldman names ignorance the most violent element in society. What would it mean if we recognized "sins" of greed, hatred and ignorance, realized the sanctity of all life, and worked protecting and preserving earth, our home?

November 3rd, 2016
Acknowledge all the good in the world

"If it were so simple. If only there were evil people somewhere insidiously committing evil deeds, and it were necessary only to separate them from the rest of us and destroy them. But the line dividing good and evil cuts through the heart of every human being. And who is willing to destroy a piece of his own heart?" (Solzhenitsyn)

True. There are very good acts by flawed wonderful human beings to whom I feel deep gratitude: Those who place the common good above individual profit and greed; who fight to save and preserve unique lands, creating national parks, forests, conservation easements; who struggle to protect air, water, earth, now in Dakota defending sacred land, throughout the world fighting deforestation, poisoning of water, exploitation; who work to save from extinction endangered plants and animals, rescue traumatized animals orphaned after poachers kill their mothers, risk lives to save ancient sites, museums, books. Doctors Without Borders who face grave danger to heal; White Helmets in Syria who rush in to find survivors after bombings; people rescuing refugees from capsized boats, who welcome those refugees; those who leave water for refugees struggling in the hot desert. Journalists and whistleblowers who witness and report what is true, whose integrity demands they speak despite danger to their own lives; our volunteer firefighters, rescue squads. The list of goodness is long.

When I see the joy in the faces of those who, after hours, find a small baby buried under rubble and still alive, who give praise to God, or the joyful tears of those who, after years of patient caring, see their orphaned animals return to the wild, or the joy of teacher, nurse or friend seeing another's healing, happiness, growth, I am touched deeply. We all know what is good — kindness, courage, care, integrity, empathy and beauty.

November 17th, 2016
There's much to fear with Trump in office

Many cheered. I and most Americans fear grave harm, the deep loss to earth (allowing pollution of air, water), to science (Trump the only international leader denying manmade climate change, promising to remove regulations, abrogate treaties, and drill everywhere). We fear closed doors to refugees seeking safety, deporting dreamers and immigrants. We fear closing women's health services, privatizing Social Security, losing health care.

What won was propaganda, false promises, repeated sound bytes ("jobs returning," "clean coal," "making America great again") and hatred, fear and violence toward "the other." Many were ignorant of how McConnell and the Republican Legislature blocked Obama's legislation to invigorate our economy, providing millions of jobs rebuilding crumbling infrastructure, repairing roads, bridges, developing mass transportation, raising minimum wage, protecting unions, regulating toxic emissions, developing alternative energies, closing tax loopholes.

Those voting for "change" by "outsiders" now can see who will rule. Since Trump's election, stocks have skyrocketed for privatized prisons, fossil fuels, military armaments. Wall Street feels confident there'll be no regulation; wealthy are confident of lowered taxes; corporations confident

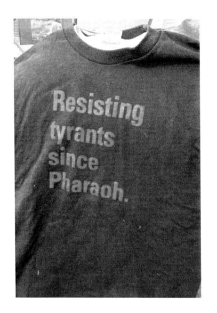

Trump's Supreme Court nominees will vote for profits, not workers' rights, for drilling, not protection of our environment, for "religion," not women's reproductive rights.. Neocons and racism have won. Democracy, integrity, fairness have lost.

Hearing Hillary this morning, I saw grace, wisdom, years of hard work for children, women, workers, families, the disabled, minorities, saw courage and intelligence and all the good she could/ would have done, thought of the vicious attacks and demonization for 30 years, the media perpetuating the idea of two flawed, disliked human beings, as if Clinton's emails equaled Trump's history of greed, lies, denigration of others.

December 9th, 2016
Pipeline protest a win for good guys

I've been inspired by the courage, wisdom, dignity of native water-protectors at Standing Rock facing brutal police power and chilling weather. When 2,000 veterans joined them as a protective buffer, my heart felt uplifted. When the Army Corp of Engineers stopped the Dakota Access Pipeline, I felt joy that truth won over corporate power. When I heard Evan McMullin, conservative candidate for president, speak of the danger to democracy in pronouncements of "I, alone," in threats to free press, denial of inalienable human rights based on gender, religion, ethnicity, in "religious freedom" used to defend discrimination, I appreciated his naming what threatens our Constitution, as I've appreciated The Post-Star's unbiased clear thoughtful reflection.

Trump has given power to the "swampy predators" he had condemned: CEOs of big banks, Exxon Mobil, coal, pharmaceutical and insurance companies, profiteers of foreclosures. He brags about removing regulations diminishing corporate profits, regulations restraining banks and Wall Street from immoral greed, regulations protecting air, water, earth, food, workers' safety, farm animals. He choses people who'd defund and privatize public schools, national parks, veterans' hospitals, Social Security, Medicare.

I want our common good: our children inhabiting a healthy, bountiful planet, want good jobs, good schools. I thought of an old Union song, "Which side are you on?" We know when water is toxic, poisoned by mercury and iron, when pipes leak, oil trains crash, when oil spills, pesticides contaminate. What side do we choose? Democracy or arrogant power, reason and fact or sound byes and fake news, a sustainable and biodiverse earth or insatiable greed threatening earth and life.

When Spanish conquistadors searched for gold, they arrogantly dismissed knowledge of native peoples who knew the earth – what plants fed and healed, where water could be found. We need to hear and heed the deep understanding of what preserves life.

December 27th, 2016
We're guilty of Budda's 'poisons'

When there's fire, flood or sickness, neighbors gather helping those in need. This holiday we speak of feeding the hungry, sheltering the poor, peace, joy, goodwill to all. How have we journeyed so far from our heart center?

Buddha spoke of three "poisons" which create suffering in ourselves and our world — greed, hatred and ignorance. In this election, those who "chose" greed got the candidate who'll reduce taxes for the wealthy and put power into big oil, coal, banks, pharmaceuticals. Those who "chose" hatred also got their man: Bannon and alt-right in power positions; rage at immigrants, Muslims, African Americans, Jews, an attorney general, Sessions, who'd hinder not protect civil rights.

I understand anger, frustration when we're not heard, fear when we feel helpless in a changing world. What I don't understand is how or why people elected Trump as their "savior" when his entire history shows someone arrogant and self-aggrandizing, unable to hear outside his own tweets, refusing to reveal or pay taxes, meet with press, read State Department papers. I don't understand workers voting for someone who is against raising minimum wage and protecting workers' rights; women voting for someone who demeans them, would deny reproductive rights, dismantle Title IX; people voting for those who pledge to privatize Social Security and Medicare, our earned safety nets. Why anyone loving clear streams, healthy lakes, good drinking water, nontoxic air, national parks and beauty of creation would "choose" unregulated drilling and coal, endangering earth for future generations.

Perhaps the greatest "poison" is ignorance — believing fake news and empty promises, not understanding cause and effect, choosing hatred over love, respect, community. It's painful to see good people cheering someone who cares nothing for their real needs. May we gather together now, as neighbors do when they see danger, protecting what's precious.

January 14th, 2017
MLK Jr.'s words are as relevant as ever

As a teacher, I know the importance to self and world of critical thinking, questioning, exploring cause and effect, seeing from another's point of view. If a student assumes s/he knows everything, does no reading or research, believes everyone else fools, I fear the closing of mind and heart, an inability to grow beyond prejudice. If a leader of a country portrays the same arrogance, refusing to hear anything contradicting his opinions, surrounding himself with people who bow to him, tweeting rather than reflecting, I fear for the country, especially if he and those around him dismantle ethical oversight, limit free press, silence and demean voices of opposition. I'm haunted by book burnings, McCarthy hearings, "good" smiling Germans saluting Heil Hitler, the danger of what Huxley calls "herd poisoning," unthinking passion fueled by propaganda and hatred. I'm fearful for democracy.

Rereading speeches of Martin Luther King Jr. for inspiration, I feel again the largeness of his being and seeing, his willingness and courage to continually open heart and mind, his deep reflection, faith and compassion–all antidotes to the greed, hatred and hollow rhetoric of our new administration. In his 1967 speech against the Vietnam War, King went beyond his moving "I have a dream" speech to draw deep connections between poverty, racism, militarism, corporate power and greed. He spoke of the danger of "those who possess power without compassion, might without morality, and strength without sight," against the "ever rising tides of hate," of the need to "undergo a radical revolution of values" in order to "save the soul of America." He warned that a "nation that continues year after year to spend more money on military defense than on programs of social uplift is approaching spiritual death." He was prophetic.

May we hear and heed his prophecy.

February 2nd, 2017
We cannot remain silent amid offenses

Trump seems to have reversed the wisdom of "how to defeat an enemy—make him a friend" into "how to turn friends into enemies." Mexicans, NATO allies, Germany, media, PBS, national parks, federal lands, refugees, immigrants, Muslims, women, people of color, scientists, EPA, those who drink water, breathe air, care about earth have become "enemies."

I remember a moving scene in the movie "Spartacus." A tyrant, hoping to kill a slave fighting for freedom, demands "Who is Spartacus?" One person after another stands up saying, "I am Spartacus." This, I think, is how we defeat immoral authority. If there's a Muslim registry, we all sign; we declare ourselves, as 400 cities have done, sanctuary cities; we welcome refugees; we stand with Standing Rock and Planned Parenthood. It's illusion to think we're safe with silence. "They" are "us,"

There's something frightening about a mean-spirited leader who advocates torture, closes doors, builds walls, attacks media, gags science, lies and is incapable of hearing anything that goes against his fragile ego. It's good to have jobs and use American-made steel. But we could use that steel repairing crumbling infrastructure, water and sewage pipes, bridges, roads, not transporting dirty tar sands or oil across sacred and public lands, endangering water, land, life. Instead of dirty coal, boom-and-bust temporary fracking jobs, we could increase the rapidly growing labor market for clean renewable energy. Instead of using taxpayers' money building a useless wall for $14 billion and investigating nonexistent voter fraud, we could meet people's real needs for work, health, home. Michigan's legislature passed a bill declaring protesters pay for police at demonstrations. But in Dallas, police gave high-fives and embraced marchers on March 21, many millions marching in peace and solidarity in the U.S. and the world. We were Spartacus, fighting for justice, democracy, our lives.

February 10th, 2017
We need to see beyond blinders

When someone loses his way to addiction (to drugs, alcohol, greed), good friends sometimes gather in love, each one speaking the truth of his actions. Sometimes a person is unable to hear, lashing out in violence. But sometimes denial breaks into awareness with the possibility for change. The man who beat John Lewis unconscious came to him with tears of remorse; Boy Scouts, after years of resistance, opened their doors to gay and transgender boys; inheritors of oil wealth gave their fortune to environmental causes, hoping to protect what their forebears exploited. And a captain of a slave ship turned his boat and life around, experiencing "amazing grace."

It is possible, this seeing the light. James Baldwin speaks of those who do not see and do not wish to see despite facts, evidence, reason, reality who stay imprisoned, accusing the world of lying, telling them "just shut up."

Republican commentator David Brooks wrote of the "Faustian bargain" made by this Congress–not seeing, not naming, not questioning Trump's lies and erratic dictatorial actions, supporting Cabinet choices, millionaires, most connected to oil, many threatening public schools, public parks and environmental, consumer, worker and civil rights protections.

It's not easy to see beyond our blinders. We need courage to change and good, caring, wise friends to show us our way home.

March 7th, 2017
Immigration gives small towns a choice

We all need work to survive, to have worth and dignity. The question: what to do when the place where we live (and often love) no longer provides work we know (and want). Families from Appalachia migrated to Baltimore and Detroit; small farms in the Midwest consolidated into industrialized farms; factories in mill towns in New England shut down; coal mines closed, unable to compete financially with natural gas, coal's pollution threatening our health and earth. People buy online harming small local businesses, and many leave for larger cities seeking work.. Change.

Towns (and cities) are challenged to find ways of surviving and thriving. Two small towns in Kansas illustrate different choices. One, Cawker City, is now a ghost town, small farms have disappeared, young adults have left. Garden City in the 1970s chose to welcome immigrants from Burma, Vietnam, Northern Africa, Mexico, other Central American countries. The town now thrives, unemployment hovering at 3 percent, an economic system of irrigated corn to feed cattle, an immigrant labor force to work in the meatpacking plants, children filling the schools. Workers produce food for export, pay taxes and rents. Restaurants, shops, schools, homes are built.

The choice for Garden City, and for us, is whether to keep out or welcome "them" into an established community. Immigration became a blessing. But it is a blessing now endangered by Trump's immigration policy and by outside "crusaders" inspired by hateful rhetoric, plotting attacks on mosques and apartments, creating terror.

The choices are ours: the illusion of safety by banning refugees and deporting immigrants, building walls, harming our farms and businesses dependent on those workers, or the reality of a vibrant diverse community, welcoming changes, promoting sustainable energy, creating local jobs, learning new skills, building mass transportation, supporting local farms/ businesses, and "welcoming the stranger who was ourselves."

April 8th, 2017
When you question familiar things

As children we accept definitions by those in authority. Even as adults we often don't question, don't look through our own eyes at our experience. Nadine Gordimer, a white South African growing up under apartheid, believed apartheid as natural as the sun's rising. So it was for many with slavery, imperialism... so it still is for many sexism and racism– acceptable norms.

It's hard to question familiar definitions: to think of "cost" of policies not just economically but in terms of our health, our water, air, planet; to define "success" not as high status and salary, but our well being, happiness, growth. And to define "pro-life" more deeply than denying women's right to choose and closing Planned Parenthood. To understand "pro-life" as recognizing and protecting the preciousness of all life: gay, transgender, refugees, immigrants, Muslim... all species ... no exceptions. Pro-life as medical care for all; preserving wilderness and beauty; keeping toxins out of air and water; education which cultivates curiosity, imagination, critical thinking, skills preparing us for good jobs, paying livable wages, doing work that doesn't endanger our health or the health of our planet; a warm home, food, community parks with swimming pools and picnic tables, national parks without drilling; libraries (like Crandall) with folk life programs, movies, supported by the national endowment of the arts.

Looking at our now Congress and president, I see the choice of death, not life. Money for weapons to kill, walls to keep out, ICE to round up, prisons to incarcerate; privatizing social security and Medicare; denying science and climate change; cutting funding for medical research, for PBS, NPR; removing regulations protecting voting, consumer rights, privacy... More money protecting and promoting corporate profits and taxes for the wealthy, less for the real needs of our common lives.

What is the real "cost?"

April 18th, 2017
The right thing is to protect and help the vulnerable

During four years of occupation of France during World War II, Le Chambon, a small Huguenot Protestant village in southern France, became a "city of refuge." Three thousand poor peasants, led and inspired by their pacifist Pastor, Andre Trocme, and other village leaders, saved 5,000 Jewish children and adults, resisting Vichy and Nazi commands. When a Vichy government official demanded a list of Jews hidden in town, Trocme replied he didn't distinguish Jew from non-Jew, but even if he had a list, he would not pass it on. "These people have come here seeking aid and protection from the Protestants of this region. I am their pastor, their shepherd. It is not the role of a shepherd to betray the sheep confided to his keeping." The chief of police threatened arrest because of his "unacceptable resistance to the laws of your country." (All quotes are from Philip Hailie's "Lest Innocent Blood Be Shed.")

Huguenots had a history of persecution. They took to heart words of the Old Testament and of Jesus, declaring themselves a "city of refuge" quoting Deuteronomy: "If the innocent are slain in a city of refuge, their duty, they believed, not only to not harm but to prevent others from doing harm, to be the Good Samaritan of Luke, following the words of Jesus: 'You shall love the Lord your God with all your heart and with all your strength, and with all your mind; and your neighbor as yourself.'"

To the villagers, it was simple, natural: If someone comes to your door seeking safety, you open the door. If someone is unjustly persecuted and vulnerable, you protect and shelter them from harm.

May we follow their example.

May 17th, 2017
How can people support such evils?

Looking at history–at the Inquisition, slavery, genocide of native peoples, imperialism, colonialism, the Holocaust, Rwanda, ISIS–one wonders how ordinary people could allow such extraordinary actions, how "evil" could feel justified, righteous, patriotic, "good." What were they thinking?

Elizabeth Minnich in "The Evil of Banality" looks at what seems incomprehensible: accepting as natural what's unnatural, as normal what's insane. The small steps leading to great "evil": to separating from other beings, denying their humanity; remaining silent –in order to not stand out, be accepted, not lose job or privilege. Accepting lies, propaganda, clichés. Not questioning. Not thinking.

How else explain cheering the new "health care bill?" Powerful Republicans not questioning or caring who loses, who benefits: 24 million people becoming uninsured in a decade with 800 billion cut from Medicaid, money for elderly, poor, families, community health services; huge tax breaks for corporations and the richest Americans; premiums vastly increased, especially for 40 to 64-year olds; "essential services" protected by Obamacare no longer required for insurance plans; prescription drugs, annual caps, hospital coverage, mental health, pre-existing condition all potentially lost; states further burdened, necessitating more cuts for needed services. This redistributing of wealth making the rich richer, the rest poorer. What were they thinking?

Even more incomprehensible is how ordinary people allow earth, our only home, to be harmed: drilling and transporting oil and gas everywhere, endangering lakes and streams; removing regulations protecting air, water, soil, wetlands; allowing toxins and agrichemicals to poison us; not seeing connections between our actions (fossil fuels, industrial farms) and rising waters from glacial melts, not seeing warming waters causing intense storms; not seeing toxic drinking water, asthma, cancer resulting from our actions, not understanding the causes of droughts, water wars, and climate refugees.

Corporate greed and power and purposeful denial and misinformation prey on ignorance and fear. The antidote: awareness, questioning, speaking out, powerful action to protect the health of earth and all inhabitants. Awareness now, rather than future remorse at allowing incomprehensible "evil."

May 27th, 2017
Every day there's a new Trump problem

Everyday a new outrage: Trump firing Comey for investigating his connection to Russia; Trump revealing classified information to Russia, endangering the source (Israel's Intelligence Service) and trust; Trump constantly lying, silencing any opposition. More disturbing than incompetence, ignorance, arrogance and lack of knowledge are his dangerous actions: drastic cuts in environmental and worker protection, national parks, science and health research, public broadcasting, community arts; opening national monuments, federal lands, sacred sites to drilling and mining; allowing access to fragile environments and increasing fossil fuel subsidies; reducing by 70 percent subsidies to renewable energies (a major job growth industry).

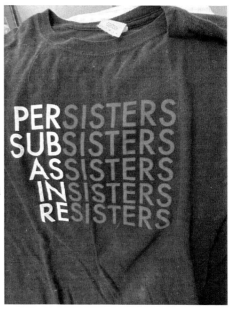

Jeff Sessions works to increase harsh mandatory sentencing for nonviolent crime and build more privatized prisons. Trump works to keep out refugees desperately fleeing war, builds massive wall, imprisons and deports immigrants who have committed no crimes, have worked on farms, in hotels and construction, paid taxes, built businesses. DeVos works to privatize schools; Medicare is being undercut in preparation for a privatized system. The new "health" care bill would deny coverage to millions. The administration continues its obsessive vendetta to defund Planned Parenthood and women's health services here and abroad, resulting in many maternal deaths.

Follow the money; every bill touted by Trump and his Congress gives more to the wealthy, fossil fuels, voices of hate, weapons. We must speak and act to protect what is precious. Einstein's "The world is a dangerous place, not because of those who do evil, but because of those who look on and do nothing," Martin Luther King, Jr.'s "We must learn that passively to accept an unjust system is to cooperate with that system and to become therefore a participant in its evil," and Edmund Burke's "All that is necessary for the triumph of evil is for good men to do nothing." All prophetic and true.

July 6th, 2017
Learning a lesson from the Great Depression

During our Depression, FDR inspired an anxious people saying "the only thing we have to fear is fear itself." He created programs to give people a sense of security and hope, helping drought stricken farmers, unemployed workers and the hungry with government programs– the CCC, WPA, Farm Program, Unemployment Insurance. He infused the economy by creating jobs, building much needed infrastructure, invigorating national parks, enriching depleted soil through conservation and employing artists to create beauty, programs not only providing needed wages, but giving pride and dignity to workers.

The question for those in power is whether to ease fear by creating programs, making people feel more secure and empowered, or increase fear, making them more compliant, passive. Our administration has, I believe, done the latter, rousing fear, anger, hate; building walls; deporting immigrants who have built a life here, raised families, worked hard; keeping out refugees fleeing danger, posing no real threat; making almost all Americans afraid of losing health care; taking money from public schools and public transportation; restricting voting claiming nonexistent voter fraud; demeaning the press, silencing protest; denying climate change, which the Department of Defense lists as our greatest terrorist threat; pulling out of the Paris agreement (one of only three countries); cheering "success" in removing regulations that protect us, our air, water, wetlands. Privatizing our common good.

Follow the money; fossil fuels, large corporations, agribusiness, pharmaceuticals, insurance and armament industries, the very wealthy. Who loses and who gains?

In fear, especially cultivated by those in power, we often blame false "enemies," not seeing real danger to life and democracy. I saw an exhibit of old Portuguese families on the Cape, photographs and stories. One man wrote how, during the Depression, everyone needed work, but as traditional "Republicans," they first fought FDR –until they saw and finally realized his governmental programs would be a blessing, would ease and enrich their lives. The importance for all of us to question and understand more deeply what really nourishes our lives.

July 25th, 2017
'Moral' agendas are only causing harm

Some rigid religious "leaders" have hijacked religion for political gain with their empty slogans: "Moral majority" is anything but moral, "pro-life" anything but "life." I watch the smiling white men surround Trump as his administration signs away protection of air and water, funding for public education, parks, science research, community services, civil rights. With arrogant carelessness for life and incredible hypocrisy, they proclaim the "sanctity of life" while being funded by forces of death: tobacco, agribusiness, fossil fuels, NRA.

Trump's "gag order" "Protecting Life" endangers the health and life of millions by blocking billions of dollars in U.S. global health assistance to poor and developing nations, not only for family planning agencies (which never used U.S. funds for abortion), but for all global health agencies: programs on HIV/AIDS, Zika, maternal and child health, malaria, immunization, nutrition…if "abortion" is mentioned. Like defunding sex education in high schools, the result: unwanted pregnancies, increased abortions, suffering and death.

Like the "gag order" forbidding NIH's research on gun deaths or environmental agencies' research on climate change, one sees the damage of political rigid ideology which harms "life."

"Religious freedom" is a rallying call. Hobby Lobby won its "right" to deny contraception coverage to employees, others declared their right to discriminate and deny employment or services to gays and lesbians– proclaiming our country was founded on Christianity, ignoring the wisdom of our Founding Fathers who knew the danger of theocracy and the necessity of separating church and state for protection of both. John Adams wrote, "The government of the U.S. is not, in any sense, founded on the Christian religion." "God" is not mentioned in our Constitution; the Declaration of Independence declares "Governments instituted among men, deriving their just powers from the consent of the governed" (not God). The words "Under God" were inserted in our pledge in 1954.

Thoughtful religious leaders know love, peace, compassion, kindness are the essence of all religion and of a diverse and thriving country. Thomas Paine wrote, "The world is my country, all mankind are my brethren, and to do good is my religion."

August 31st, 2017
It's criminal to not protect environment

I was heart-moved by the devastation and losses of so many in Texas and by the courage, caring and kindness of rescuers. But I felt heart-sickened that "once in a hundred years" disasters now happen frequently, predicted by all who understand cause and effect: the damage of paving over wetlands and creating canals for uncontrolled oil drilling in Louisiana, destroying natural flood protection; of "explosive" development, crumbling infrastructure, no zoning regulations amplifying Houston's tragedy; of Petro continually contaminating poor communities now spewing millions of pounds of toxic pollution. We know or should know global warming causes stronger winds, larger storm surges, melting glaciers, flooding, that warming oceans intensify storms, record heat causes droughts. The "news" shows disastrous flooding, not mentioning "climate change" or that one-third of Bangladesh is under water, over 1,000 people dead; or that Sub-Sahara Africa is becoming unlivable, intense heat destroying crops, animals, livelihood. MIT's report predicts over one billion climate refugees fleeing uninhabitable lands, food and water scarcity, violence. What aren't we thinking?

The media is complicit in silence and the President and Congress culpable in climate denial, putting corporate profits and fossil fuels above life, allowing drilling everywhere, removing regulations protecting streams, rivers, drinking water, withdrawing from the Paris accord, and recently revoking Obama's federal standards demanding infrastructure take into account flood and storm risk management– making roads, bridges, sewage, water infrastructure climate resilient. Why are we continually shocked at predictable catastrophes and continually privatizing and making profit from tragedy?

On Oct. 1, Crandall Library is showing "Age of Consequence," a comprehensive look at why our Defense Department views climate change a terrorist threat requiring urgent action. It is criminal to refuse to see "natural" disasters as partially a consequence of human exploitation and greed, and to not take action protecting earth, our only home, by reducing fossil fuels, preserving forests and wetlands, developing renewable energies.

October 14th, 2017
We must denounce Trump's behavior

Republican Senator Corker recently spoke about the danger of Trump leading us into a World War III: his words/ actions toward North Korea, decertification of the Iran Nuclear Deal, withdrawal from the Paris Climate

Accord, irrational tweets and erratic behavior. That danger is echoed in "The Dangerous Case of Donald Trump," a just-published book written by 27 psychiatrists and mental health experts assessing Trump's unfit mental state and their "duty to warn about his narcissism, paranoid personality disorder, antisocial personality, inability to embrace anything beyond his own self."

Most of the world sees clearly his lying, bullying, bizarre behavior. The question is why some refuse to see and name what is obvious. Some clearly "stand by their man" out of self interest. He gives them what they want: unregulated corporate profits (fossil fuels, pharmaceutical and arms industries); a health bill and tax bill benefitting the very wealthy and harming the health and income of most of us in New York state; and rescinding regulations that corporations find "burdensome" which protect our lakes from acid rain, our streams, water and air from toxins, our workers (from injury) and consumers (from fraud). Under the banner of "religious freedom," discrimination against gays and lesbians is protected; patriarchal power asserted, and women's control over their own bodies limited.

My question is not how unfit and dangerous he is, nor how, for some, greed or religious ideology supersedes life and morality, but rather how some citizens, local representatives, party leaders still support someone who endangers our environment, community needs, moral values and well-being. Where do our politicians stand? Why are so many silent? And where do we stand?

"In a democracy," Rabbi Heschel, a civil rights activist, said, "not all are guilty but all are responsible."

October 28th, 2017
At polls, be loyal to what you believe in

Thoreau wrote that it is only when we get lost that we really look around; otherwise, we follow the old route, habitual and familiar. We hold on to opinions and ideas handed down to us by family, church, those in power. But sometime education and life allow us to see anew, beyond the blinders we were given-—to question old beliefs, to analyze cause and effect, to understand actions and their consequences. To think critically.

Senators Flake, McCain, Dent, Corker, all Conservative Republicans, thought critically about their own party, fearful of where their party has gone under Trump—the lies, bullying, demeaning, threatening, the racism, ignorance of foreign policy, withdrawal from the international community, loss of respect by other nations. They spoke of the complicity of those in their party who are silent, fearing loss of huge corporate funding, of Bannon's nativism and rhetoric, and of an electorate energized by bigotry and hatred. Once a party of principle, many acting in a bipartisan way, especially on environmental issues, they feared their party had lost its moral center.

December 2nd, 2017
As voters, we must be as fair as jurors

I was recently called for jury duty. At first I was reluctant, but later felt honored to be part of a justice system gathering diverse community people, asking potential jurors to listen closely to the judge and to the law and to assume innocence until proven guilty. Two questions to the jury made me think: "How do you know if someone's lying or telling the truth?" and "What one word would describe you as a jurist?"

In terms of the first, I'd answer: I'd look at evidence, facts, history, consistency; would listen to bipartisan, objective witnesses; would determine who would lose and who would win from testimony. In terms of the second, all potential jurists answered "open-minded and fair."

In a democracy, we are all jurors, each trying to judge who's guilty of doing harm and who is innocent. I think of these "guidelines" with political issues. Some issues are complex, but some are clear. Hearing people rail against "liberals," I look up "liberal" in the dictionary: "broad-minded, tolerant, not bound by authoritarianism or orthodoxy. One who is open-minded." Isn't that what we, potential jurists, should be?

December 20, 2017
The powerful are addicted to greed

Opioid addiction is a recognized epidemic, but there are other epidemics so interwoven within a society that they feel almost natural, accepted. Rape, domestic abuse, harassment, exploitation, and discrimination against women have all been part of unquestioned patriarchal power, the seeing of women as object rather than subject, a male's entitlement and privilege.

Other societal "addictions" are seen as signs of success, not symptoms of sickness: our addiction to greed, to having more, no matter the harm caused by our actions. Surely something is wrong with those already having much more than they need aggressively fighting for more money and power to feed their addiction. And something is terribly wrong with those elected to serve the common people continually enhancing that power and greed, promoting a tax "reform" giving huge tax breaks to corporations and the obscenely wealthy, taking money from CHIP, medical expenses, Medicaid, Social Security, education, science, infrastructure, national parks, everything precious to life.

Recovering addicts say addicts will rob their mother to satisfy their addiction. That is what the addiction to greed and power do–narrow our mind so that we view everything and everyone as objects for exploitation, feeling no ethical qualms about drilling, mining, dumping toxins, destroying our mother earth, no matter the cost to future generations.

There is a children's lawsuit arguing the constitutional rights of young people for a livable planet, arguing the need to limit carbon and methane emissions to reduce global warming. The evidence is there: record heat, terrible droughts, ice caps melting, warming waters, flooding, growing intensity of wildfires and hurricanes, climate refugees seeking to live. Some countries, like Ecuador, have declared "the rights of water," "the rights of earth." Our Supreme Court, on the other hand, has ruled that corporations are "people" and declared the rights of corporations.

It's heart-sickening to see people cheering those who are addicted, who demean and exploit and harm our earth. It's ethically bankrupt and criminal for those in power to enable and enhance that addiction and its destructive power rather than heal our society's moral sickness and suffering.

January 30th, 2018
Prejudice– a cycle of hating the 'other'

We all have blinders closing off what is clear and visible to others–world views we've inherited from family and culture, opinions shaped by the media, prejudices fed by those in power.

During the celebration of Martin Luther King Jr., I viewed again newsreel photos: small black children holding hands going into elementary school, a single black girl walking to a high school, young black people  sitting at a restaurant counter, sharecroppers trying to vote, poor people marching peacefully carrying signs "I am a man." And I saw white people with Confederate flags and Nazi insignias in Alabama, Mississippi, Boston, Chicago screaming, spitting with venomous hatred, swinging bats, saw police with dogs, water hoses, batons. On one side courage and goodness and on the other ignorance and hatred.

It's the same story of power, abuse, destruction throughout history; white people "naturally" assuming superiority and privilege over people of color; men assuming superiority and control over women, feeling it is their right to sexually abuse, demean, exploit them; imperialist countries assuming it is their right to rule over another's country, exploiting that country's wealth, imprisoning and repressing its people; humans exerting their right to drill, dig, poison, exploit living earth. A sense of superiority and entitlement, an inability to see others as living beings deserving dignity and respect, committing acts of cruelty, violence, greed, while calling the "other" inferior and savage.

I'd love to find people in those newsreel photos screaming their hatred (and fear) of black people, their patriotic pride in colonial oppression, their arrogance toward women. I would like to ask them if years and experience have enabled them to finally see the fullness and dignity of the "other," feel remorse, grow in understanding, rather than remain entrapped in hatred and destruction. It is always "amazing grace" to move from blindness to vision, from constriction to openness—to feel the richness, depth, beauty of "the other" and of our now aware self.

84

March 7th, 2018
Guns in classrooms is not a solution

I'm inspired by the courage, passion and honesty of students and I am dismayed by the cowardice of Florida senators unwilling to even take up debate on the issue of gun violence, Republicans repeating NRA clichés about "freedom" and "good men with guns." It was bizarre seeing a smiling Trump talk about the beauty of teachers carrying concealed weapons, horrifying to hear thunderous applause. If more people having more guns would make us safe, we'd be the safest country in the world instead of the least safe: 18 school shootings since the year began.

A teacher educates. A gun in her/his pocket couldn't stop someone whose semi-automatic kills 17 people in five minutes. Rifles for hunting, guns for protection, school protection procedures are reasonable, but why this rage against what clearly would protect life: banning assault weapons and implementing comprehensive background checks which stop those who endanger life– domestic abusers who commit 50 percent of terrorist acts, white racists spewing hatred, men with records of violent instability?

Students ask what we should all ask representatives: Who funds you? Whose side are you on? If you really wanted children safe, wouldn't you increase rather than cut funding for education and community mental health? Protect air we breathe, water we drink? Support maternal and children's health? Support rather than suppress NIH research on gun violence?

Instead of listening, NRA's LaPierre rages against journalists' "fake news" and calls students "paid protestors" destroying our country. Some governors threaten arrests. Clearly NRA demands total loyalty from those politicians they fund.

Throughout history, good people have joined together for justice. Crandall Library will be showing four inspiring films "In the Public Interest" about communities rising up against gun violence. On March 24, there will be a "march for our lives" in Washington and on April 20 a National High School student walkout. May we march, walk, fight for our lives.

May 6, 2018
We should make our world a better place

The narrator in Fitzgerald's *The Great Gatsby* says: "I saw that what he had done was, to him, entirely justified. They were careless people, smashing up things and creatures, then retreating back into their money, their vast carelessness, whatever it was that kept them together, letting other people clean up the mess they made." Abusive privilege/power not caring for our lives, for earth, for our future, selling public lands to oil, gas, drilling, removing regulations protecting water and air, giving to those who have too much, taking from those unable to live a healthy, dignified life. "Letting other people clean up the mess they made.'

Antidotes to carelessness, greed and complicity are acts of care and integrity: young people in Parkland, Chicago, Albany, Glens Falls, their passion, intelligence, courage in naming the fanaticism of NRA, holding politicians responsible; teachers in West Virginia, Tennessee, Oklahoma, Arizona, demanding more public education funding; Black Lives Matter with the MeToo movement speaking truth to power; journalists risking life to photograph, document, investigate abuses of power; whistleblowers revealing corruption; indigenous peoples protecting water and sacred land. All remind us what is precious: respect for all living forms.

In his apostolic exhortation, Pope Francis spoke of "saints next door" more pleasing to God than "religions elites" who are "the enemies of holiness" "forcing others to submit to their myopic absolutist interpretations," reducing Jesus to "cold and harsh logic... bereft of true love," a "sinister ideology absorbed with social and political advantages" poisoning us with "the venom of hatred, ruthlessly vilifying others." The "proper attitude," according to the Pope, is to "stand in the shoes of brothers and sisters risking life to offer a future to their children."

We could all be everyday "saints" leaving our children and our earth a bit better through our care, love, and kindness.

May 19th, 2018
What kind of world would we all choose? Questions

We all have beliefs, opinions, political parties, religious ideologies, some of us grasping them tightly, as the Rev. William Sloane Coffin says, more like a "drunkard clinging to a lamp post for security rather than for illumination," imprisoned in our secure familiar world.

But if we viewed experiences without blinders, what would we see, what would we choose? A loving family or an abusive family? Parents, teachers, politicians listening to real needs or those imposing their will through power? Beings treated with respect and dignity or subjected to bullying, denigration? A livable wage or not having enough to feed, house, clothe our family? Clean water to drink, clear air to breathe, or toxic water and polluted air? Birds, mountains, oceans, biodiversity or land and waters exploited, bereft of life? Protection from fraud in banking, school loans, real estate or no restraints on corruption and unjust power? Integrity and honesty or unrestrained greed? An ability to grow to our fullest potential or face obstacles based on poverty, race, gender? A world of care and understanding or one of power and violence!

What gives our lives meaning? When do we feel joy and connection? What would we want said about us as individuals and about our country?

If we went into our heart, how would we answer these questions? What world would we choose for ourselves and our children?

June 29th, 2018
Administration is unethical, anti-life

In schools, we have workshops preventing bullying, teaching children to listen, empathize, work with others; we encourage honesty, respect, kindness; we ask children to look closely, research, understand cause/effect. To think. To question. My question: How can people support a president who does what we wouldn't want in our children, spouses, neighbors? How did the Republican Party lose its reason and ethics, cheering a "leader" whose policies do not make America great but make America isolated, disliked, feared, our country withdrawing from the Paris Climate Agreement, the UN Human Rights Council, the Iran nuclear deal and from our allies? If we are "taking America back," it's to racism, Jim Crow, voter suppression, religious dogma.

What is their plan of action: deny climate change; restrict voting rights; build walls and private detention centers for children; limit women's reproductive rights; give huge tax breaks to the wealthy and corporations; limit consumer protection from fraud; remove regulations protecting clean air and water.

I understand those consumed with greed choosing these policies, but why do workers support a party that limits unions and collective bargaining, doesn't fight for a livable wage, denies health care, undercuts safety nets? I understand anger, but why against refugees and immigrants fleeing violence, why against poor people struggling to live, instead of against those responsible for suffering?

What will really make us "great" and good?

August 9th, 2018
Dangerous shifts happen gradually

I'm haunted by photos from the Holocaust: an insane leader worshiped by "good" people, their arms raised in "Heil Hitler," smashing the windows of Jewish shops, approving Nuremberg "laws" limiting where Jews could go, closing their eyes to the extermination camps.. In Rwanda, friends killing neighbors with machetes. In Sarajevo and all over the world people killing those with whom they once lived. How, I wonder, are "good," kind people roused to acts of cruelty they'd never have imagined?

The answer: gradually.

Trump supporters threaten, cheer, laugh, and are silent when he attacks journalists and election workers; calls immigrants rapists, criminals, and invading vermin; when he encourages violence and attacks anyone who is not totally loyal. I see a "leader" preparing his followers for that movement from caring to cruelty and violence. I see his party smiling in support, getting what they want from their complicity or bowing in fear of his power.

When local "tragedies" occur fire, floods, sickness, we show caring. We're now witnessing devastating "natural" disasters every year: killing heat, devastating fires, warming oceans, flooding. Care is important, but it is not enough. Refusal to act on scientific evidence of global climate change increased by using fossil fuels is criminal. The real terrorist threat is not refugees fleeing, not immigrants working here, but deliberate cultivation by this administration of racism, ignorance, greed, violence.

Einstein: "The world is is a dangerous place, not because of those who do evil, but because of those who look on and do nothing" MLK: "We must learn that passively to accept an unjust system is to cooperate with that system, and thereby to become a participant in evil."

August 30th, 2018
We shouldn't listen to those who harm us

Seeing workers, women, good people cheering this president, I wonder: why/how could you cheer someone who demeans, bullies, threatens, demands total loyalty, who appoints people selling our public lands and waters to highest bidders, who works against workers' rights, environmental protection, who would do us harm?

For some it's the second amendment: "no one is going to take away my gun." But no one is taking away guns. For years there was a ban on assault weapons, supported by 77 percent of Americans and by Ford, Reagan, Carter. I think of my small rescue dog surviving in woodlands, fiercely protecting food I just gave him, me saying: you can have your food, I don't want it, and me saying to those protecting their right to bear arms,"no one is taking away your guns."

For some it is "pro life," a fierce vendetta against women and their control over their own body, the patriarchal desire for power and control

For some it is simple rage: at two people who, loving each other, want to marry; at trans people just wanting to live their authentic lives; at immigrants fleeing violence; at people of color just wanting justice and equality, wanting to live their lives with dignity.

What is the fear and anger that makes people cheer someone who gives them nothing but rage and hatred against another?

October 12, 2018
Fight for good of the people, not PACS

Throughout history, power and privilege have used name-calling (ignorant housewives, angry spinster, violent mob, left wing socialist) to silence those fighting for simple justice: workers striking for better pay, African Americans marching for civil rights, Chicano farm workers for fair wages, women for birth control and reproductive choice, protesters against war in Vietnam, against environmental pollution, destruction of native lands, for limiting fossil fuels and mitigating catastrophic climate change. Those same privileged voices yelled "socialism" with Medicare, Medicaid, Social Security, Obamacare. They've used "right to work" to destroy unions; privatization to undercut public education; "freedom of religion" to deny women reproductive choice. They've demonized "big government" to destroy necessary regulations protecting air, water, earth, life.

Recently McConnell self-righteously lambasted "mobs" and left-wing Democrats for blocking Kavanaugh's nomination, he, who only hours after Scalia's death, declared any appointment by Obama, the sitting president, null/void, refusing to even process the moderate, impeccable Garland for the Supreme Court, now refusing to hear reasonable objections to Kavanaugh's partisan diatribes, allegations of sexual misconduct, ideological judicial decisions against reproductive choice, environmental regulations, workers' rights.

The Supreme Court's "Citizen's United" allowed unlimited, undisclosed dark money to poison democracy. PACs, naming themselves "Americans for Progress" and "American Traditional Partners," used their billions to lie, create fear, work against anyone not supporting their agenda. Follow their money to see their lackeys. In Republican primaries and general elections, they target thoughtful, caring, independent candidates who do not adhere to their demands. Too often their money loudly broadcasting their lies determines the outcome of an election.

Here, in the North Country, we have a real choice: Tedra Cobb for Congress, Emily Martz for state Senate–people with integrity who would protect Social Security, support health care for all, women's reproductive choice, livable wages, public education–people who have lived in and worked in our community, fighting not for wealthy PACs but for our common good.

October 26th, 2018
Misogyny, colonialism use of power

It's not a question of "he said/she said," but of a clear, terrifying pattern of patriarchal power throughout history and throughout the world which views women as objects, not recognizing their rights, dignity, personhood. If one out of three women experiences rape and violence, if between 40 to 70 percent of women experience abuse and harassment, we need to not only judge a perpetrator but a whole culture that defines as "normal" denigration, objectification and violence against women. Denis Mukwege, recently awarded the Nobel Peace Prize for devoting his life to defending victims of sexual violence in the Democratic Republic of Congo, spoke of the terrible brutality against women in his country. But clearly misogyny is not localized. It is a toxic world epidemic.

In one class, I asked male students to list what they were taught/told as boy children about acceptable behavior. Their answer: boys/men hould be tough, powerful, winners; they shouldn't be vulnerable, cry, display emotions, except anger; should not be a sissy, a faggot, sensitive. Looking at the list, one student said, "This is pathological."

I see Trump, a powerful bully demeaning women, as an example of that male pathology. It's horrifying to hear him cheered and especially painful to hear women cheering.

White Europeans in their colonial conquests displayed a similar inability to see those in developing countries as precious human beings. Imperialism– denying people's rights, culture, language, exploiting land and resources for greed–seemed natural, normal, good. That arrogance/ ignorance is replicated in our attitude toward our earth: poisoning water and air, destroying forests, wetlands, species, using and exploiting resources for our wealth without recognizing the uncredible diverse life and beauty.

This arrogant narcissism, this inability to recognize the dignity and worth of another, shrinks mind, heart, soul. Not a question of "he said/she said," but a moral blindness causing great suffering, endangering all life.

December 11th, 2018
History– looking behind to see ahead

In "Why History Matters," Gerda Lerner writes about the importance of remembering history to understand, acknowledge, and learn. Looking at our now Mexican "immigrant crisis," I think of our history– the war on Mexico (the Spanish American War) giving us New Mexico, Colorado, California, Nevada, Utah, Arizona. Americans were the "illegal aliens," violently seizing land where Mexicans had lived for generations, Kit Carson and our "heroes"were murderers of Mexicans and Indians.

The now immigrants seeking asylum are fleeing violence partially precipitated by our government's past actions in Central America protecting United Fruit and our economic, military interests. In 1954, the CIA's covert operation deposed democratically-elected Guatemalan President Arbenz and his program of promoting liberal democracy: supporting minimum wage, universal suffrage, land reform. Dictatorships, civil wars, violence followed. In Honduras, we backed military dictator Garcia and were silent when democratically elected President Zelaya was overthrown in a coup by Velas-quez, graduate of School of the Americas, a U.S. Army training program. Organized crime took hold, cocaine shipments started, people began fleeing. In El Salvador in the 1980's our country played an active role in its "dirty war," supporting the Salvadorian military in its human rights abuses.

Howard Zinn wrote "A People's History of the United States" recording stories almost absent from traditional historical texts: government's abuse of power and people's continual inspiring struggles for justice and freedom. He wrote, "When government, media and institutions select certain events for remembering and ignore others, we have the responsibility to supply the missing information." Denying historical truths, we eliminate our ability to learn, to become active in shaping our future. We make heroes of those who did harm and blame those who fought courageously for the good.

Zinn writes, "Just to tell untold truths has a powerful effect, for people may then ask, what shall we do?"

January 15th, 2019
Loyalty can blind us to harmful reality

It's strange when we're unable to recognize actions that clearly harm us and others, following leaders working against our well-being. How do we not see what others see so clearly?

I think of powerful leaders becoming objects of worship, able to mesmerize followers, spouting outrageous lies despite mountains of contrary evidence, demanding total loyalty, naming all who disagree stupid, monsters, terrorists. They're not accountable for their actions; they refuse to disclose personal finances; have no ability to hear another, to question; see conspiracies against them, call them "witch hunts"; name themselves the only source for truth.

Clearly this describes our now president and the danger he poses. But it also speaks to the blindness and/or willing complicity of his loyal followers. I think of the scientific world consensus around human-made climate change and its catastrophic consequences for future life.

We now experience warming oceans, extreme flooding, disastrous wildfires, intense hurricanes, death of wildlife, of coral reefs, of life. Glaciers are melting more rapidly than predicted,

CO_2 emissions are increasing, our way of life clearly threatened if we don't act. Yet the president of our country, the highest emitter of greenhouse gasses, denies what almost all people and nations recognize. Trump would increase our production of coal and fossil fuels, allowing more drilling in oceans and wetlands, more toxic pollution of air and water, remove the very regulations and restraints that could limit the grave danger of climate change. In ignorance and greed, we commit suicide and homicide.

I think of Jonestown and its mass suicides, of dangerous cult "leaders" and loyal believers following their leader to their death. We have signs outside our homes: "drive like your kids live here." I think: live and act as if you and your children live here on this earth, our only home.

January 26th, 2019
Immigrants aren't the real threat to U.S.

It's true, there's a national emergency, but it's not immigrants at our borders. It's true there are dangerous criminals threatening our lives, but they aren't immigrants, refugees, Muslims. Throughout history, demagogues and tyrants rouse anger against the wrong "enemy" as a way to distract from real causes of real pain (see PBS' The Dictator's Playbook).

Overwhelming research reveals the grave danger of climate change: wildfires, floods, droughts, farm lands no longer viable, water undrinkable, climate refugees. A recent report demonstrated the great impact of climate change on our health: infectious diseases, asthma, tick and insect diseases, allergies. mental illnesses, heat-related death, mercury, toxins.

Who's criminal, who's responsible? Oil companies and large corporations lying about connections between fossil fuels and climate change; government complicity allowing federal lands and waters to be mined, water and air to be polluted; pharmaceutical companies disguising opioids' addictive and deadly effects; arms traders making money off killing innocents. For greed, people kill. The war isn't on coal but on facts, on poor people, women's reproductive health, our earth. Criminals are in high cabinet positions: Mulvaney (refusing to protect consumers); DeVos (not supporting public education); Zinke sacrificing public lands to drilling; Pruitt and Wheeler (fossil fuel lobbyists) heading EPA. Income inequality grows: the richest 1 percent earns over 50 percent of the world's wealth. Profit over people; we all pay the cost.

Four people were sent to prison for leaving jugs of water in the desert. Those responsible for poisoning Flint's water haven't been charged.

Martin Luther King spoke of the "appalling silence and inaction of good people," saying "The time is always right to do right." Issues are complex, but sometimes it's simple to see what is "right," to act: to see the real national emergency, real criminals; to thank whistle-blowers risking lives to reveal real crimes.

March 23rd, 2019
Minorities want a seat, not the table

We all partake in small "innocent" lies. But there are deeper lies causing great harm: cigarette companies, pharmaceuticals, fossil fuels, pesticides purposefully disguising known dangers to increase huge profits. More dangerous, political lies about actions by the CIA and our government overthrowing democratically elected leaders in Iran, Guatemala, Chile, supporting right-wing dictators, involving us in wars. Even deeper, more pervasive, are historical and cultural lies, so large they seem immutable, seem true. Nadine Gordimer, a white person growing up in apartheid South Africa, spoke of assuming apartheid was natural, like the sun rising. So it was for many during the days of slavery or imperialism/colonialism, many believing it moral to enslave and rule over other "interior" people. So with patriarchal power throughout history, cultivating the illusion of male superiority as if it were "the truth"

The #MeToo movement exposed the extraordinary extent of violence against women: The number of American women murdered by male partners between 2001 and 2012 was 11,766, double the amount of casualties during war. Rape, sexual harassment, trafficking, violence against nonwhites, Muslims. Jews, refugees, immigrants, lesbians, gays are epidemic. Cruelty against animals accepted.

When I hear "Jews will not replace us" or hatred of Muslims or immigrants, I see hate but, even more, fear. I want to say no one wants to replace anyone; everyone just wants a seat at the table, to be treated with respect, dignity. The loss of white male human privilege is not a loss of self, but of privilege based on illusion of superiority; not "natural," but cultivated to keep privilege, power. Exclusion, discrimination, oppression aren't marks of "excellence," but of deep ignorance.

Questioning what seems "natural," recognizing lies, breaking free of illusions– those we tell and those we believe– is liberating. Not loss but growth, allowing us to experience our true connection to self and others.

April 4th, 2019
Military spending steals from all of us

Trump's proposed budget seems an April Fool's joke: give more to those who have too much, take from those with too little; make cuts in Medicare, Medicaid, Supplemental Nutrition Assistance, cuts in agencies dealing with environmental protection, state and USAID, housing and urban development, agriculture, interior, health and human services, education, energy, labor, justice. Increase spending in defense, a space missile program (similar to Reagan's failed "Star Wars")and build more walls.

Our military budget is already huge, 54 percent of our discretionary spending budget, outspending the combined military budgets of the next seven largest countries. We are the largest exporters of weapons, supporting Boeing, the arms industry, wars around the globe.

What really enriches and protects our lives? Healthy communities, good jobs, education, health care, good air, water, parks, beauty, wildlife, protecting our homes and lives from continual "once in a lifetime," "catastrophic" flooding, hurricanes, droughts, wildfires. Not the illusion of security through walls, but policies building infrastructures; not expanding mining and drilling, but supporting renewable energy.

General Eisenhower saw clearly the danger of the military industrial complex, its terrible cost: "Every gun that is made, every warship launched, every rocket fired signifies, in the final sense, a theft from those who hunger and are not fed, those who are cold and are not clothed. The world in arms is not spending money alone. It is spending the sweat of its laborers, the genius of its scientists, the hopes of its children." Endangering a livable earth for all beings.

Trump spoke of the "support of police, the military," "tough people" who "don't play it tough until they get to a certain point, and then it would be very bad." A threat of violence and the use of power. Fascism continually chooses weapons, violence. The Bible offers us a choice between life or death. Let us choose life.

April 23, 2019
People in power use mocking to persuade

Teaching Composition in Great Meadow prison, I read a narrative by an older Vermont student writing about her experience in second grade when a teacher mocked her enthusiastic painting of a snowman, hung up her drawing and said that is not what a snowman looks like. The student never painted again. An inmate responded: "That teacher should be in prison. She murdered the spirit of that child." He was right.

I think of individuals mocked throughout history: Jesus, Gandhi, Martin Luther King Jr.; Programs mocked: FDR's New Deal, Social Security, unemployment insurance, Medicare, same sex marriage. I think of actions mocked: "housewives" protesting Love Canal, women speaking against abuse, indigenous people blocking pipelines, Catholic workers spilling their blood to protest nuclear arms, students fighting for sensible gun legislation. The now target for mocking is the Green New Deal. Listen to talk radio and many Republicans repeating the same scripted words.

Those that mock aren't debating ideas or facts. They use power to ridicule, attack. They fear the truth spoken by those they mock will be heard. It's almost inconceivable that our leader and his subservient minions use power to deny the catastrophic effects of climate change despite all scientific evidence about glaciers melting, oceans warming, flooding and wildfires, drought, intense hurricanes and tornadoes, climate refugees. They use power to go against what all nations and almost all people see as possible extinction of our way of life, enthusiastically fostering drilling, mining, removing protections of wetlands, oceans, air, water, undercutting sustainable and renewable resources. Endangering all life.

Thoughtful people are struggling to find a way to protect and preserve Earth, Medicare for all, good jobs, education, social justice, fairness. They are mocked by those in power who would sacrifice all life for their profits and greed. My student in prison was right: they are criminals.

Our challenge: to continue working for a liveable and flourishing world for all.

June 4th, 2019
Control over women's bodies and over our earth

I don't understand this vendetta against women, Republican State Legis-latures closing Planned Parenthood, restricting women's rights to their bodies and reproductive health, self-righteously declaring "dignity" of the fetus but not valuing children and women. Nor the hatred against immi-grants, refugees fleeing violence, the obsession with walls, deporting people living and working decades in our country, arresting people providing water in the desert, denying rights to homosexuals and trans-people … as if these actions would make us safe.

There is so much real need that could make our lives more secure and livable, why is this Republican Party obsessed with hatred of "the other," denying the most obvious danger to our lives and the lives of our children: climate change? How could anyone feeling the "preciousness of life" not care about our earth, not hear "dire warnings" of climate emergencies, the "catastrophic" danger to life, not see the "historic" and "unprecedented" and now frequent wildfires, intense storms, tornadoes, continual flooding, droughts, not recognize the one million species threatened with extinction, loss of biodiversity and pollinators essential to life.

In their obsession with control over women's bodies and the fetus, how do people in power not hear young people insisting governments act to save their future, our "leaders" calling methane "freedom gas," praising CO2, subsidizing fossil fuels, Pompeo viewing melting Arctic ice as wonderful, enabling us to drill, mine, excavate, exploit oil gas, rare earth minerals, sanctioning drilling everywhere, including our public lands, suppressing scientific evidence, isolating us from world consensus on the grave threat to life and need to act immediately.

Control over women's bodies, over earth, a sense of entitlement, terrible dangerous ignorance, power and greed that cannot see the rights, worth, value of all life, the deep interconnections, a mystery far beyond our limited perception.

June 13th, 2019
A leader should always possess neighborly traits

I believe most of us would agree on what we would want and/or expect of a neighbor, friend, parent, teacher, leader. Of a neighbor, we would want someone who is friendly, respects us, helps when there is danger, does not threaten, trespass, poison or harm us or our property. We would want a friend able to hear, support, be compassionate and truthful. With a parent or partner someone who would encourage us, would not insult or demean, and a teacher who respects and listens, encouraging each student to grow into their fullest self. I believe we would want leaders who are conscious, thoughtful, able to work with and hear others, accept wisdom based on experience, who would not silence ideas, not fire those who speak what is truthful. And I would like to believe we would want in our own life to grow in understanding, to have integrity, to feel, at the end of our lives, that we did what we could to make ourselves and our world better.

Clearly there are people who bully, threaten, demean, lie, who see themselves as the center of the universe, who assert their will and power. The great problem is when someone we would not want as friend, neighbor, parent, teacher, is the President of the most powerful country in the world, threatening the world, asserting his will, making others afraid of his power, doing great harm to body and spirit. I don't understand how many cheer someone who exhibits traits we would find unacceptable in those around us, who is an embarrassment, dangerous to our country and the world, how many choose not to see what is so obvious.

July 27th, 2019
Small blue Earth is fragile, in danger

Astronauts spoke of our small blue Earth seen from space, a tiny fragile planet in a vast universe. How could people not see the grave danger to our beautiful blue Earth? May we all "go home" to our heart and deeper knowing.

August 17th, 2019
Racism, Sexism, Imperialism– all delusions allowing us to control other beings

Mental illness causes suffering to individuals and families. But there are historical and cultural mental illnesses so pervasive they feel "normal" and going against these norms "crazy." They are based on the delusional belief that one group is superior to another and is therefore justified in exploiting and oppressing those "inferior."

We all can be taught to see something as good, patriotic, noble which is clearly wrong: the killing and taking land from native peoples, colonizing another's land, exploiting the resources, denying the rights of inhabitants. Slavery, the buying and selling of human beings, lynching, rampages of the KKK–all seen by many as natural and even good.

When I see newsreels showing black people simply trying to vote attacked by hoses and dogs, or people screaming hate and spitting at young black children going to school, when I see the dignity of nonviolence during the Civil Rights movement, I wonder how anyone could see the white race as superior, see a person of darker skin as inferior. And throughout history and throughout the world, how, I wonder, have men maintained their illusion of superiority while sexually harassing, raping, exploiting, controlling women's bodies and actions, doing acts of violence with impunity, as if it were their "right." These mental delusions are rampant, easily ignited by dangerous leaders. They are fed by fear, hate, greed and power, fed by ignorance.

When privilege and power are questioned, those in power often feel victimized, threatened. But what is lost is unwarranted privilege and delusion, not one's essential being.

When I taught Ellison's "The Invisible Man," a student said: "If you take away someone's illusions you kill them." I remember going home and thinking whether that was true. What I think and believe is the opposite really: you free someone to grow into their deeper self, returning them to an authentic life and what is true.

September 8th, 2019
New thoughts to add to 'questionnaire'

It's important to think, understand cause and effect, listen– not just block thought and words with a bullhorn. It's important to question both ourselves and others.

In his poem, "Questionnaire," Wendell Berry asks: "How much poison are you willing to eat for the success of the free market and global trade? How much of our beloved land are you willing to desecrate? List mountains, rivers, towns, farms you could readily do without." To that list, I add, what would you sacrifice—our ocean, clean water, clean air, trees, animals, birds, bees, wildflowers, beauty, incredible diversity of life—what relinquish for greed?

Is integrity, kindness and caring important in your world? And how could you support a president who can't not lie, who threatens and bullies anyone disagreeing, demanding total loyalty, who dismisses science, is incapable of listening to others, who is arrogant, cruel, heartless? Is it to protect your 401K, to get more money? How much would you not see, not hear, not care, remaining silent, complicit with immorality and cruelty? Is Democracy important to you, and fairness, and justice for all? What would you answer your children, grandchildren and great-grandchildren when they ask about history, science and overwhelming evidence of climate change: small islands and coastlines destroyed by floods, catastrophic violent hurricanes, wildfires, "historic" catastrophes now common, extinction and loss.

Did you not care? Not hear about warming waters, melting glaciers, droughts, climate refugees, extinction of species, about permafrost dissolving, about our reaching a tipping point if we do not stop our consumption of fossil fuels, stop deforestation, reduce methane? What was more important to you than preserving a livable home for the future generations? And what would we want said about us and our lives when we die, about our actions and inaction when the world was in such danger?

September 28th, 2019
Refreshing to hear debate on issues

Listening to the debates of the Democratic candidates for president, I thought how good to hear thoughtful discussion about real issues affecting our lives: climate change and possible paths to limit catastrophic harm to our planet; social justice and criminal justice reform; sensible gun policies; medical care as a human right; immigration reform and paths to citizenship; education, racism, infrastructure, raising the minimum wage, economic inequality. A rich discussion with differences between the candidates. The only issue missing from the discussion was cultural misogyny– the prevalence of rape, domestic violence, denial of reproductive rights, inequality at so many levels and the connection between patriarchal power, gun violence and war. But still I felt good. Finally we were having deep and meaningful discussions.

I felt the same goodness hearing young people marching for their future, speaking forcefully and so articulately about real solutions to catastrophic climate change – the necessity of limiting our energy uses, our exploitation of the earth; the need to develop sustainable alternative energies, to keep fossil fuels in the ground; the power of corporations to buy politicians and shape domestic and foreign politics. They understood climate refugees fleeing droughts, floods and catastrophic storms, the poor and vulnerable the first victims of climate change, the developed and powerful countries most responsible for this climate emergency. The need to act now.

In the past I could imagine such a debate within the Republican Party, discussing limited government, reducing debt, protecting earth. Now, however, loyalty to Trump seems to be their only platform. What would they talk about: How high and wide the wall? How to remove more regulations protecting earth, air, water? How to limit women's reproductive choices? How to limit voting rights? How to protect their leader no matter the cost to our democracy.

December 1st, 2019
Where have Republican principles gone?

A friend's daughter was mesmerized by her cult leader. Her friends saw clearly the grave danger of her "leader": abusive, tyrannical, arrogant. No one could convince her. I thought of Johnstown, of people following their guru, even to their death. I couldn't understand, just as I can't understand Trump's loyal followers, willing to support him despite his arrogance, lies, harassment, cruelty, firing anyone questioning his will, accusing all of "fake news," "witch hunts," "lynch mobs," praising his greatness, demeaning whistleblowers, calling immigrants criminals, scientists and decorated military officers and distinguished officials ignorant "nonTrumpites," as if the only qualification for "truth" was total loyalty to him, no matter what he did. In the 2016 primary, the other Republicans, demeaned by him, were "not Trumpites." Now, however, all are silent, fearful Trumpites.

Trump's favorite leaders are tyrants: Putin, Duerte, Balsanaro, Erdogan, Saudi Arabia – all criminals. I think of our precious Democracy, of Earth, life, all that is precious now threatened.

Declaring his own greatness, demeaning whistle blowers, calling immigrants animals, and dismissing scientists and decorated military officers as ignorant. Demanding total loyalty. In the 2016 primary he demeaned all the other Repubicans. Now they are all silent, becoming faithful, fearful Tumpites.

January 23rd, 2020
President poses risk to our lives

Issues are complex. With more facts and evidence, we sometimes see more deeply, change views. Sometimes, however, it is more a question of values and how we choose to act –with integrity or with greed. Do we choose to dump dangerous toxins in water, air, earth? Do we mine, drill, harm wetlands, parks, rivers, streams, sacred areas? Do we limit voting rights of people? Refuse to negotiate pharmaceutical drug prices? Pass a tax bill giving billions to banks and huge corporations? Are repeated words "fake news," "witch hunt," "lynch mobs," "hoax" effective? Is threatening and firing anyone disagreeing or refusing to allow documents or witnesses helpful to truth? Are facts, science, critical thinking important for democracy? What would you want said about what you did or did not do in your life? What Earth would you want your children to inherit?

James Baldwin speaks of those. who do not see and do not wish to see. Of "willful ignorance." How else explain our president and the loyal Trumpites not seeing what is so obvious: climate extinction. The floods, droughts, intense storms, wildfires, the record heat, loss of birds, bees, mammals, climate refugees fleeing uninhabitable homes.

And how could Republicans not see the integrity and courage of all those who testified at the hearings about Trump's complicity in Ukraine? How could they not question his refusal to have witnesses, the withholding of vital documents, accusing everyone who is a truth teller of lying.

The red flag law is used to remove dangerous weapons from those who pose great risks to life. This president poses great risks to our lives.

February 6th, 2020
We should fear losing democracy

I'm not a fancy White House lawyer but some things are obvious: How can any Senator deny calling witnesses for a trial, especially when testimony is relevant to the situation? How can they deny obtaining documents imperative to finding that truth? And how can a lawyer actually say, as Dershowitz does, that even if the president is guilty, he has a right to do what he wants if he feels it is in the best interest for the country? And why do almost all Republicans sit like zombies, denying what is clear?

If it's fear, clearly their "leader" threatens retribution for dissent, a mark of a tyrant demanding absolute obedience, their silence and complicity a loss of integrity. They should be deeply ashamed.

McConnell has held up hundreds of bills passed by the House, bills speaking to real needs of our lives: education, health, environment, meaningful jobs, livable wages. Instead of legislation helping us to live healthy lives, Republican state legislators focus obsessively on bills limiting women's reproductive choice and birth control, building ineffective walls, denying immigrants the right for asylum in their state, allowing ICE to deport people who have lived and worked honestly in their communities for decades.

What is this vendetta against women, immigrants, the poor, against gays, transgender people, this undercutting children's healthy meals, limiting medical care for those with green cards, while allowing toxins in water and air?

February 10th, 2020
Restriction and Denial

 Thirty-one states want to restrict education, passing laws, banning books, threatening teachers. Twenty-one states have enacted voter suppression laws-limiting polling places, gerrymandering, giving Republican legislatures the ability to overturn voters' will. Congressional Republicans voted against the "Freedom to Vote Act," a bill easily passed 98-0 for decades, the party has clearly changed.

 Trump repeats his big lie of a stolen election, while attempting to steal the election he lost. He pressures state legislators to find votes, election officials and Pence to deny certification of results, federal agencies to seize states' voting machines. He stirs his admirers to storm the Capitol. The RNC calls the Jan. 6's violent insurrection "legitimate political discourse." Trump and Maga threaten all who honor their oath to the constitution and tell the truth in testimony. Senator Romney courageously says the truth: "Shame falls on a party that would censure persons of conscience who seek truth in the face of vitriol.

 Shame on Trump, Stefanik, Republican Party. The Party has clearly lost any ethical and democatic center, cheering hatred, mob violence, and abusive power. Rabbi Heschel, who walked beside MLK, said, "Not all are guilty, but all are responsible."

March 5th, 2020
The President is a dangerous bully

In school we teach children not to bully, to be respectful, to listen. Yet, we have as president a most dangerous bully: demeaning, threatening, and firing anyone not following his commands: firing Vindman and Sondland for courageously speaking truth at the impeachment trial; denigrating Flake and McCain; threatening Romney and Schiff; firing scientists reporting on climate change and historical preservation; condemning staff who attempt to save important documents from shredding; calling Gallagher, a war criminal, a "hero"; pressuring Barr to change Stone's sentencing. Honest, long-time workers resign in protest or are fired. Trump surrounds himself with fawning loyalists.

Senate Republicans are silent and complicit, not willing to restrain this paranoid bully, New York Republicans and Stefanik shout spirited approval of all Trump says and does. Trump, in continual revenge, punishes New York state for allowing immigrants to have driver's licenses, condemns states and cities for lessening emissions or giving sanctuary.

Trump's proposed budget gives more and more to the wealthy, a bloated defense budget, nuclear armaments in space, a useless wall to ICE. The budget cuts children's food programs, education, medical care, and programs protecting air, water, earth.

I think of us in the school yard, classroom, workplace and how we respond to abusive power, to good people being bullied, demeaned, to children and women being abused, to people suffering environmental toxins. Do we choose to not see? Is our 401K more important than protecting our earth from environmental catastrophe? Do we yell approval when Trump blames the poor, immigrants, refugees, women, Democrats, socialists, environmentalists, scientists, journalists as the "enemy," inspiring rage against wrong "enemies," inciting violence, as did the followers of Mussolini and Hitler?

I fear "innocent and good" people cheering him, ignorant of history, science, economics, democracy, and disconnected from empathy and simple morality.

April 9th, 2020
Despite horror, we can learn from this

There's much suffering with the corona pandemic–sickness, isolation, fear. But it's not foolish to see what we can learn from this and any unwanted event.

We are forced to stop our habitual motion: our air and water are cleaner, steams once dead flow with fish. My neighbor who walks our wilderness road every day saw no planes overhead and said: The Earth can now breathe. We can breathe. Values can become clearer with loss.

I go out with bird seeds and read my car's bumper stickers: "Live simply that others may simply live"; "The earth provides enough for everyone's needs but not man's greed" (Gandhi); "We are all in this together."

April 23rd, 2020
Grateful for those who show courage

When I see corruption, arrogance, cruelty, abusive power, I wonder how they get away with it. McConnell and Republicans blocking "vote by mail," claiming nonexistent "voter fraud" while purposely purging voters from the rolls and closing polling stations, using dark money.

How does the EPA and this administration use the COVID-19 pandemic to remove regulations protecting us from mercury, toxins, car emissions, pollution of air and water? And how, I think, don't people see the danger of Trump.

Clearly nothing matters to those in power– no evidence, facts, reasoning, morality. I think of the "trials" of black Americans in the Jim Crow South, all-white juries finding a black person guilty despite all contrary evidence, or finding white men innocent who have clearly murdered people of color. Or women who have been harassed, beaten and raped—tried for murder and sent to prison for defending themselves. Or any rational person seeing the destruction of our Earth—global warming, melting glaciers, floods, drought, wildfires, extinctions—denying the clear dangers to our home.

But I also think of those throughout history who see clearly, who risk their lives working for justice, human rights, earth rights, who do kindness and goodness in small and great ways, and I ask: How do they do it, show such courage?

May their names be an inspiration, their lives a blessing.

May 7th, 2020
Bad politicians are nation's worst virus

One doesn't need a crystal ball to predict the present and future "priorities" of this administration. Because of the coronavirus epidemic, we gave necessary money to those in need but gave even more to large corporations and businesses. On the insistence of Democrats, money was directed to hospitals and medical care but states, like NY, in terrible economic distress, were denied funding for police, firefighters and teachers, McConnell telling states to declare bankruptcy, accusing them of reckless spending, not acknowledging that New York is a major giver to the federal government, McConnell's Kentucky a major receiver.

In a "reasoning" which is ncomprehensible logically but clear politically, abortion was listed as nonessential, regulations protecting air, water, emissions were rescinded, doors were closed to refugees and those seeking green cards. Meanwhile, the wall continued to be built and meat-slaughtering plants were ordered open (by the defense authorization act) because "essential," and workers refusing to return and undocumented farmworkers were unable to collect unemployment.

The coronavirus was and is real, dangerous, but those using it for greed, power, and control are much more dangerous.

June 13th, 2020
Trump only threatens, does not listen or learn

Trump, sounding like any dictator, told state governors, "You have to dominate, if you don't dominate you're wasting your time. They're going to run over you, you're going to look like a bunch of jerks. You have to dominate... You've got to arrest people... Put them in jail for ten years and you'll never see this stuff again."

Florida Rep. Gaetz tweeted, "Now that we see Antifa as terrorists, can we hunt them down like we do in the Middle East?" And Sen. Cotton spoke about "no quarter for insurrectionists, anarchists, rioters, and looters."

I think: who are these "leaders" of our country and who do they declare "enemies of the state"? The right wing violent racists carrying guns and swastikas? Corporations polluting, poisoning air, water? No, the target of their rage are the hundreds of thousands of white and black people here and around the world asking for simple justice, peacefully protesting police violence against George Lloyd and the hundreds of innocent black men and women killed by police or imprisoned unjustly, protesting the grave injustices of systemic racism in jobs, medical care, education, voting, housing, environmental toxins poisoning their neighborhoods.

The "terrorists" are not those demanding justice, but heavily armed soldiers and police equipped with military gear violently attacking them with tear gas and rubber bullets and the politicians inspiring and encouraging that violence.

When a chief of police asked protesters what they wanted, they said, "join us," and he did. Some police applauded protesters, taking the knee showing support. When people are heard and respected, when real needs are met, people are not violent. But Trump can only rant, blame, threaten, has never been able to listen or learn, can only use power to fire, terrorize, control, dominate.

July 28th, 2020
'Good trouble' is good

John Lewis spoke of "good trouble"-- protesting when you see something unfair, unjust. I think of his peaceful march from Selma to Montgomery for voting rights, the police and sheriffs with whips, dogs, batons, horses rushing at them, Lewis beaten to almost death; of courageous Black people sitting at a counter in Woolworths, freedom riders, sharecroppers trying to vote, small Black children attending school, a Black student trying to attend a state college. I see white people raging, screaming hatred, and I think, what did these peaceful protesters want that seemed so outrageous to those filled with hatred: to vote, have good education, be treated with respect, be seen as human beings with equal rights.

Lewis, a short while before his death, joined the BLM march, his last "good trouble" Trump responded with force, sending officers with tear gas to clear peaceful protesters in Washington D.C., sending federal agents to Portland, Chicago, Albuquerque to fight against "violent anarchists allied with the radical left Democrats attacking the legitimacy of our institutions."

Trump follows a clear script: criticize the press, create an "enemy," use violence to create fear." To him, all looting and violence should be punished. But Tom Ridge, the country's first director of Homeland Security under George W. Bush, warned: "the department was not established to be the president's personal militia... It would be a sad day in hell before I would give consent to a unilateral, uninvited intervention into one of my cities." In Chicago, the "wall of moms" cried: "I don't see no riot here, take off your riot gear, Feds stay clear, moms are here," waving hands above their head singing "Hands up, please don't shoot me." Peaceful. "Good" trouble.

August 16th, 2020
What is valued by Republicans?

Politicians use name-calling to misrepresent/destroy opponents. Under Trump and his loyalists, including our Representative Stefanik, there is a barrage of hate against "left wing democratic liberals," "radical socialists," "violent terrorists and protestors" who seek "to destroy our democratic institutions."

As a "liberal" who supports Social Security, Medicare, Medicaid, unemployment insurance, I wonder what Republicans stand for. They attacked Obamacare but never proposed any real alternatives. They talk about working people but have never voted for raising the minimum wage, child care, a job program. They talk about no deficit spending but passed a tax bill benefiting the very wealthy, dramatically increasing our deficit. (Only under Clinton have we balanced our budget.)

Republicans used to speak about defending our country and democracy, but are now totally silent about overwhelming evidence of Russian interference in our elections and have engaged in a purposeful campaign to limit voting rights: close down polls, remove registered voters, claim mail in voting as "voter fraud," defund the Postal Service. The U.S. ranks the highest in Covid deaths, but there is no federal leadership around Covid: a lack of testing; revengeful vendettas against all who speak the truth if it challenges Trump's attacks on medical experts, scientists. And always conscious willful lies and misinformation about the grave dangers of climate change.

Republicans speak of "violent protesters." I see people peacefully demonstrating for a true democracy for equal rights for people of color, women, workers, immigrants, the environment being met by violent police forces sent by Trump in the name of "law and order." I fear Trump's dictatorial power and the racist, misogynist white supremacists repeating Trump's diatribe against "invaders." I fear their hatred, violence, and ignorance.

Emma Goldman: "The most violent element in a society is ignorance."

September 10th, 2020
Systemic violence is all around us

We hear a lot about looting, violence, abuse. I'd like to expand the definitions to 'legal" crimes," not punished: looting through tax loopholes; political bribery for political favors; exploitation of workers; dark money buying politicians to serve their interests, their greed.

Violence to property is harmful, but the violence done to our earth (through exploitation, oil spills, mining, drilling, deforestation, toxic pollution) is legal and subsidized. Wars, that pathology of violence, is often honored.

Some abuse is so integral to cultures it's considered "normal." The acceptance of patriarchal power, whether by Taliban or religious fundamentalists or by husbands or bosses, allows for sexual and physical violence, control over women's bodies, economic discrimination, unrecognized misogyny in attitudes and behavior. Systemic violence against Blacks – in education, economics, health, housing, medical care, laws – goes unnoticed by many whites.

White supremacists and neo-Nazis, often quoting Trump, have committed mass killing of innocent people at Walmart's, music festivals, churches and synagogues.

At the Republican Convention, countless speakers shouted about fear and danger, the need for "law and order." They meant, I think, the fear of white people, not the fear of Black people throughout our history who have been lynched, imprisoned, murdered – the fear they experience every day of being killed in their homes, cars, street by police unable to see their humanity.

With tears, one Black man said: We have always loved America, but America has never loved us.

October 8th, 2020
Our country needs a big wake-up call

Many of us can deny the obvious. Sometimes evidence, experience, reason don't matter. Still, I can't understand Trump supporters denying climate change with wildfires devastating the west, fires in Siberia, catastrophic coastal storms in the Southeast, droughts, record heat, people believing Trump's "it'll get cooler," believing "climate change is a hoax," not question Trump's deregulation of companies polluting our air, water, wetlands. Believe Trump about elections rigged, scientific evidence flawed, medical experts ignorant? Believe moderate Biden a left-wing anarchist and Barr calling peaceful protests seditious? Not see that "pro-life" doesn't mean pro-life for all–child care, medical care, food, housing? How not see the danger of white supremacists using Trump's words to kill innocents in churches, temples, Walmart? Not question Trump threatening, firing anyone challenging his lies, his autocratic authority?

In a letter from "Conservative Christians for faith and democracy," I read hateful propaganda about "radical socialist left-wing Democrats" destroying our country, a repeated script Stefanik echoes. No mention of faith, democracy, no words of Jesus, the Pope, the prophets Jeremiah, Isaiah, Amos, no words about compassion, feeding the hungry, poverty, war, suffering, injustice, or the dignity and worth of all beings, no words about protecting God's creation.

I think of inspiring words of true spiritual leaders: Rabbi Herschel, Martin Luther King, Rev. Barber, John Lewis, the courageous history of indigenous people risking lives to protect earth, of women, blacks, immigrants, the poor proclaiming our lives matter.

The Jewish High Holy Days are a time to reflect on our actions, where we have "missed the mark," how we can become more conscious, compassionate, caring human beings. The blowing of the shofar (the ram's horn) is a wake-up call-to return to our hearts, atone for harmful actions, heal ourselves, repair our broken world.

Ruth Bader Ginsburg died on Rosh Hashanah. May her work for justice be our wake-up call.

The time is always right
to do what is right
– Martin Luther King, Jr.

October 10th, 2020
U.S. threatened by danger from within

I have disagreed with many Presidents: about the Vietnam War, invading Iraq, polluting waters, tax cuts for the wealthy, attempts to privatize our safety nets and defund Social Security and Medicare. But I have never feared, as I do now, the loss of democracy because of dangerous words and actions. Trump might not literally poison like Putin, but he poisons through conscious constant misinformation about COVID-19 and climate change, threatening/firing all who disagree, surrounding himself with loyalists.

He cannot listen, blames everyone, cannot accept responsibility. Because he will never accept defeat, he tries to undercut voting, declaring mail voting fraudulent, elections rigged, saying even before the next election he will not agree to accept results of voters. He and his powerful corrupt cronies close and/or drastically limit polling stations, throw out ballots of eligible voters, raise what's essentially a poll tax, reject repeated bipartisan investigations of Russian hacking. Trump has asked his followers to question and intimidate voters at polls.

Proud boys and white supremacists have their man. Trump and Barr talk about antifa as a terrorist group but the FBI sees no evidence of antifa and strong evidence of a growing threat of white racist violence–shootings in churches, synagogues, Walmart, murderers echoing Trump's words of hatred, his call for his "good people to go to cities with guns to "save" democracy.

I don't know how my good, kind neighbors can vote for someone wanting total dominance. Perhaps because of greed and tax breaks? A rigid religious fundamentalism seeking to undermine what our Founding Fathers saw as essential– the separation of church and state? Perhaps believing propaganda the right wing has used for decades about "law and order" to silence legitimate dissent? Perhaps wanting power, like Representative Stefanik, supporting Trump no matter his danger?

November 21st, 2020
Support for Trump is inexplicable

As someone who respects our human ability to question, to think deeply and critically, I'm always shocked by our human capacity to deny what is obvious: to call the devastating wildfires, catastrophic hurricanes, flooding, droughts, warming oceans, melting glaciers, extinctions, global warming and climate change a "hoax," the deadly COVID-19 virus spreading as "not serious." Trump claiming mail-in votes fraudulent, the election stolen, he the winner– despite all bipartisan election officials, governors, district attorneys, court findings declaring this election the "most secure in American history" with no evidence of cheating.

Not conceding to what is obvious, to admit loss, Trump undercuts voting, the essence of democracy. And he endangers–refusing to allow Biden to receive briefings and funding necessary for a smooth transition of power. More than 150 national security offices see this delay "as a serious risk to national security." Those with integrity have left his administration or been threatened or fired for "disloyalty."

What is shocking is not his totally predictable lies, narcissism, cruelty, but the silent and often verbal complicity of most of his Republican loyalists, including our representative Stefanik, not naming or restraining the danger. Even more horrifying to me is how so many people believe his words despite all evidence, logic, reason. Trump may feel himself chosen by God or that he is God, but how could so many "good people" believe him, support him, collaborate? Look at those leading his denial: Guiliani, Alex Jones, QAnon Greene, Roger Stone, the Patriot Boys, white supremacists, neo-Nazis…

And by what strange manipulation and propaganda did justice, equality, medical care for all, raising the minimum wage, protecting air and water, preserving earth, Black Lives Matter, wearing masks, science, biodiversity, caring, kindness... become the "dangerous enemies."

December 12th, 2020
Tracing how we got to this very low point in our politics

The first president I remember was Eisenhower. Moderate, thoughtful, he raised taxes on the wealthy (taxes of 91%), lowered defense spending, warned of the military-industrial complex and was the only Republican to balance our budget. The two parties differed, but compromised.

I'm not sure how "government" became the "enemy." FDR's New Deal and Johnson's "War on Poverty" "promoted the general welfare." Social Security, Unemployment Insurance, Medicare, Medicaid, federal funding for education, Head Start, the Civil Rights Act, air pollution and water protection...all moved our country toward a more just society.

Under Reagan's "trickle down" tax theory, inequality and the deficit grew. Taxes were lowered on the wealthy and on large corporations. Collective bargaining and union rights were limited, military spending increased. The deficit continued growing under Bush — more corporate welfare, more tax breaks for the rich, a growing inequality amplified with Trump's tax "reform." Regulations protecting air, water, citizens' rights were removed. Strident calls urged martial law and the overturning of the election.

With Falwell's Religious Right, the Tea Party, Citizens United (allowing unlimited dark money in politics), with Newt Gingrich's conspiratorial theories, name-calling, tirades against "socialists, communists and Democrats destroying our country", and with Republicans pledging to never compromise, the stage was set for Trump.

Somehow, regular people believed equality, justice, domestic programs were dangerous communist plots and that we needed more "law and order." There were no longer two parties, but a god-king demanding total loyalty, threatening, firing all who questioned his power—Republican and Democratic election officials, medical doctors, scientists. Strident calls urged martial law and the overturning our election.

With COVID-19 raging, Trump's base protested masks, health warnings. White supremacists created terror. Seemingly "responsible" Republican senators became silent, complicit, collaborators afraid to alienate Trump's violent base. And many of us, including me, felt fear for our country,

January 16th, 2021
Dangerous words preceded the attack

Painfully obvious last Wednesday was the violence of mobs storming our Capitol, like Kristallnacht in Nazi Germany, like Brownshirts, like the KKK, threatening death. But it wasn't just thugs on the ground. Trump's tweets about voter fraud, a stolen election, his winning by a landslide stirred followers into a rage to "save our country."

Marching with Trump were his obedient enablers in Congress, repeating lies, questioning Biden's presidency, warning of liberals, Democrats, socialists plunging our country into chaos, willfully and deliberately ignoring the real danger of this autocrat demanding absolute power, condemning news as "fake," threatening and firing anyone questioning him, his mob shouting "kill Pence!"

Trump's danger has been very obvious for years, a danger most Republicans in the Senate and House chose to ignore, echoing his lies, supporting him, and now seemingly surprised at the obvious consequences of his words and actions. Above Trump and the Republicans are the corporate sponsors and and "below" are his loyal voters, all complicit.

Our Representative Stefanik has been a willing collaborator in the violence. She mildly condemns that violence but not the precipitating cause, staunchly justifying her attempt to overturn the election, repeating stale propaganda about liberal Democratic socialists overthrowing democracy. She self-righteously condemns Twitter's silencing of Trump as violating free speech, calls Governor Cuomo the "worst governor ever," and consistently supports her man, never speaking of his incompetence around COVID-19, his lies and threats, or his seditious call for his followers to overthrow democracy.

Both Trump and Stefanik are incapable of acknowledging and/or apologizing for the dangerous consequences of their words and actions. From Trump's violent speech to the violence that followed, Stefanik has been a very willing collaborator with domestic terrorism. My question is if those voting for them are able to see the danger unleashed?

February 6th, 2021
Condemn those who supported violence

"Paranoia involves intense anxious or fearful feelings and thoughts often related to persecution, threat, or conspiracy. Paranoia can become delusions when irrational thoughts or beliefs become so fixed that nothing including contrary evidence can convince a person that what they think or feel is not true."

No matter how much evidence that this presidential election was fair, that Trump spread a lie about fraudulent votes, that Trump is an autocrat wanting power, those that follow him believe him "their savior," someone fighting a secret pedophilia ring and the "dark state."

When I watch newsreels showing the savagery and violence of slavery, lynchings, Jim Crow laws, of police and dogs threatening people trying to vote or peacefully marching at Selma, or jeering with hatred at Black children trying to attend school or a Black person moving into a white neighborhood, I wonder how those committing violence could possibly hold the illusion of "white supremacy" when everything indicates white fear and hatred.

If a neighbor was threatening violence against me, brandishing a gun, I'd want my good neighbors to intervene, to restrain the threat. But if they not only affirmed but cheered the delusional one, I would be horrified as I am now, by Republicans in power who condemon violence but threaten those in their own party who, with courage and integrity, speak what is true and do not condemn those who threaten to kill colleagues or who carry guns into the chamber.

One may never be able to convince those entrapped in delusion screaming "save our children" to recognize what will really save our children, our health, our earth, democracy, justice. But it feels important to name and condemn the complicity of those legislators – Cruz, Hawley, Stefanik – who, for profit and power, rouse violence through their deliberate lies.

February 23th, 2021
Patriots follow their conscience

It's not even hidden. Republicans say to win elections they must restrict voting. They shunned and threatened all not totally loyal to Trump, those following their conscience. I think of the seven courageous Republican senators and 10 representatives who voted their conscience, voted to impeach, the courage it took, their integrity. I kept thinking, "how could others not see" what is evident? Then I remembered the Jim Crow South–the all white juries finding a black man guilty with no evidence, or a white man innocent who clearly killed a person of color. The facts unimportant. The inability to see beyond the blinders, beyond loyalty, beyond fear and prejudice, beyond power.

When the Supreme Court gutted parts of the Voting Rights Act, some states where Republicans controlled the legislatures rushed into high gear, limiting voting access, demanding identity cards, purging voter rolls, gerrymandering districts. But many worked diligently—registering voters, establishing early and mail-in voting, making voting accessible to all. Their hard work worked. More people voted in this fair election than ever before. But still the big lie, people raging that the election was stolen, threatening election workers, attacking the Capitol. What was really "stolen" were reason and morality.

March 9th, 2021
GOP attacks but stands for nothing

Anyone seeing Republican Senators at the gathering of "conservatives" (aka: loyal supporters of Trump), would find them quite bizarre, almost funny – their gestures, standing ovations, speeches filled with "sound and fury, signifying nothing"– if they weren't so dangerous. No vision, policies, ethics, only threats against disobedience, lies about stolen elections, and condemnation of "radical" evil Democrats.

Meanwhile those "evil" Democrats are working on The American Rescue Plan" – money for vaccine distribution, for states and cities devastated by COVID-19, for our schools, fire and police departments, for an extension of unemployment benefits; for stopping evictions, for $1,400 for those earning under $80,000, for child care, for small businesses. All necessary to restart our economy and allow people to survive.

Biden has also introduced legislation to rebuild our crumbling, underfunded infrastructure, rated C – for roads, bridges, water and sewage systems – focusing on green energy and, at the same time, creating good jobs. In Congress, Democrats are proposing, again, H 1, passed by the House but blocked from a Senate vote by McConnell, a bill reinstating provisions of the 1965 Voting Rights Act, curbing dark money and partisan gerrymandering, increasing both voting rights and voting security.

All good, one would think, if one thought at all of people and democracy, "The American Rescue Plan" supported by 77% of Americans, mayors and governors, economic experts. Yet most Republicans (including Stefanik) have pledged to block these bills, focusing instead on suppressing votes (43 Republican state legislatures passing bills restricting rather than expanding voting rights), "rigging" the election to "win," praising their "golden calf," their false idol obsessed with power and greed.

In the 50's, Senator McCarthy chaired the "House UnAmerican Activities Committee," accusing and destroying innocent lives with lies about "saving us from Communism." Finally stopped in 1954, someone said what I'd say now to loyalist Republicans: "Haven't you done enough harm? Have you no sense of decency?"

March 25th, 2021
Preserving Earth is not elitist work

When Republicans called the Green New Deal "elitist," AOC responded, "Tell people in the SE Bronx suffering from asthma it's elitist." I add, tell people whose drinking water is toxic with mercury and lead, those in poor neighborhoods suffering increased cancers, those who cannot fish after toxic oil spills. Tell those suffering from intense and frequent hurricanes, wildfires, flooding, who have lost homes, lives. Tell farmers where drought and floods have destroyed crops, farms becoming dust bowls. Tell refugees fleeing homes they love because they're unable to grow food, farmland becoming desert.

What's the cost of losing bees, pollinators and our crops, fruit, trees, flowers dependent on them? Of losing birds and butterflies through toxic pesticides. Of coral reefs bleached, oceans acidified, plastic destroying ocean life?

Even if we only defined "cost" in terms of money, the cost of global warming is immense, trillions of dollars every year. The deeper loss is our precious home.

It is true that there is real and painful loss for those dependent on the jobs fossil fuels provide, and that we need to create alternative jobs in green energies, schools teaching new skills, retraining. During the Depression, FDR created the Civilian Conservation Corp. Our infrastructure is under-funded, crumbling. What would it mean to build our country by creating a Civilian Climate Corp as Biden has proposed in his infrastructure bill, creating good jobs, skills, livable wages for workers displaced by change, building our country, economy and a sustainable Earth?

For the air we breathe.
For the water we drink.
For the places we call home.

The "elite" are not people just wanting to live their lives, but the fossil fuel industry wanting to expand its power and profits, subsidized heavily by our taxes, maintaining power through dark money, paying politicians to do their bidding. It's not elite to understand inter-dependency, cause and effect, to protect our homes from destruction, to preserve for future generations a world of beauty and bounty.

May 13th, 2021
Embrace Earth and all that is precious

How do thoughtful caring people become cruel, unthinking, believing absurdities and committing atrocities. Nazi Germany, Rwanda, cults, Isis and here, believing Trump won the presidency, Biden a pedophile, climate change and COVID-19 a hoax?

Biden thoughtfully creates programs he (and I) believe help people: controlling the pandemic, extending unemployment, stopping evictions, expanding health care, child care, paid family leave, helping essential workers, opening schools safely, creating good-paying clean energy jobs, building crumbling infrastructure; proposing the wealthy pay their fair share, increasing the current 21% tax to 28% (lower than the 35% before Trump's tax cut benefiting the wealthy); reducing carbon and methane emissions, combating the climate crisis.

Republicans' main political strategy: to scoff, restrict voting rights, limit women's reproductive rights, deny rights of trans, gays. Why would anyone cheer those caring so little for them?

To McConnell's "100% of my focus is on stopping this new administration," Jill Psaki, Biden's press secretary, responded, "I guess the contrast for people is 100% of our focus is on delivering relief to people and getting the pandemic under control."

Republicans' main strategy for electoral victory is not conservative ideals but loyalty to Trump, threatening all dissenters. Cheney, and a small remnant of conservatives with integrity, know the danger: "Republicans must decide whether we are going to support truth and fidelity to the Constitution." They warn, "Republicans must steer away from the dangerous and anti-democratic Trump."

For loyalty to democracy, Cheney is voted out of her powerful position, Stefanik ambitiously stepping in to join those who've sold their souls for power, echoing Trump's big lie, endorsing another recount in Arizona, questioning the voting system and democracy. Voltaire said, "Those that can make you believe absurdities will make you commit atrocities."

June 19th, 2021
The risk to democracy

I watch "True Believers" cheering preposterous conspiracy theories, storming our Capitol, stirred by an arrogant narcissistic autocrat obsessively repeating the election stolen and promising to save our country from immigrants, socialists, democrats, from "the swamp." I watch Republican loyalists stirring fear, hatred, delusion, suggesting a military overthrow, citing nonexistent voter fraud. I see Republican legislators passing laws restricting voting rights, gay rights, rights of women, using partisan gerrymandering, censoring dissenters.

Scholars, studying democracies falling prey to dictatorships, warn "our democracy is now at risk!" I wonder how and why would people "choose" dictators, relinquish freedom?

Observing Nazism's rise, Fromm writes in "Escape from Freedom" (1941): "If the meaning of life becomes doubtful, if one's relations to others and to oneself do not offer security" there is temptation to "surrender freedom to dictators." Anxiety, fear, aloneness..., the "lust for power ... rooted in weakness... the inability of the individual self to stand alone and live!" Fromm sees clearly why some choose a dictator and violence: "The more the drive toward life is thwarted, the stronger is the drive toward destruction…Destructiveness is the outcome of unlived life."

The answer to dictatorship: a country that enables us all to live a life of meaning, of value and worth and dignity.

June 20th, 2021
Knowledge of past enriches present

The question is not "good" or "bad" but true, deep, rich, complex, whether looking at the history of our family, our culture, or our nation. I think what it means to revise, see again, expand beyond the "innocence" of a created history constructed by those in power to an expanded sense of the real "story."

I think of a student who saw in the family's attic incredibly beautiful paintings of her great-grandmother she had thought "crazy" Another who had never known her grandmother died in an illegal botched abortion. I think of so many women who, limited by societal constriction, could not live their full lives, limited by poverty, abuse, internalized self-hatred. I think of all the lives we never knew.

I, a graduate student in literature, had read almost no literature by women, people of color, immigrants, knew so little about women's history, black history, workers struggles, almost nothing about the sacred knowledge of indigenous people viewed as "savages" and slaughtered, never learning what they could have taught us about the gifts and wisdom of our mother earth.... Or the struggles and protests of coal miners, farmers, workers, veterans fighting for equality, justice. Or of the secret CIA actions against elected leaders in Central America, Haiti, Africa... our government propping up dictators to protect corporate interests.

With historical knowledge, there is a loss of romanticized "heroes" and myths about the past. But we can be inspired and moved by new "heroes," always there and still here, fighting for justice, freedom, truth, the moral good, now our possible teachers, inspiring us with their courage and beauty. I think of the movement now to silence critical thinking about the past, willful denial and willful ignorance to preserve a past that never was, preventing us from a future that could be for ourselves and our country.

July 15th, 2021
Recognize what is good and what is bad

It's insane that we wouldn't protect water from mercury, lead, plastic, protect air from toxic pollution, protect children from poison. Seeing raging wildfires, killing heat, devastating hurricanes, floods, droughts ... how could we not do everything to protect our only home? How not see through the obvious propaganda calling child care, medical care, education, livable wage, justice, sustainable earth as "socialist," not see unrestrained greed and power as the impetus for removing regulations protecting air and water and lowering corporate and individual taxes. Not see the suffering of poverty, racism, injustice.

Shouldn't we recognize suppressing voting rights as wrong, unAmerican? Our last election, according to all the Republican and Democratic election officials and the courts, was free of any fraud, the high turnout a victory for democracy. How not question Republican legislatures desperately working to change what worked for all into one working just for them, threatening dissenting voices, questioning the election, calling Jan 6's violent insurrection "normal tourism," the whole Republican party, even in the North Country, supporting a cruel, corrupt demented man in his whining fantasies of having won? It is crazy and dangerous, dangerous as the lie that vaccines are a government plot (despite 99% of those dying of COVID are unvaccinated), teaching our complex history "unAmerican," being asked to wear a mask a terrible affront.

When someone is caught in delusions, good friends gather to speak truth, helping a friend see more clearly. "If you see danger, tell someone"..."Drive and live like your children live here"...We do live here and there is danger. Red flag laws are supposed to remove weapons from those who are dangerous. But if people support those who are dangerous, support weapons in harmful and insane hands, our country, children, earth are in real danger.

August 3rd, 2021
Police testimony was powerful

Hearing Capitol Police Officers describe their experiences on Jan. 6, I was touched by their emotional honesty, their caring and their courage in defending the Capitol, elected representatives, their comrades, and our democracy against violence and overwhelming odds.

Terrorists/insurrectionists beat them with sticks, flagpoles, furniture, using Tasers, yelling obscenities, racist slurs. The police officers spoke of physical and mental trauma but even more about the pain at the denial and indifference of Republican legislators they were defending, many of whom proclaim support of "the blue," many "too busy" to even listen to the hearings, calling it partisan play-acting, the insurrection Pelosi's fault. They were scoffing, ridiculing, dismissive—like arrogant teenagers. Had they, and those who still support Trump—despite recorded tapes showing his attempt to change election results, his threats, corruption — been living in Germany during Hitler's rise, I can see them cheering Hitler, refusing to hear the Nuremberg trials, scoffing at survivors, calling the Holocaust a hoax.

When I see people screaming at teachers trying to protect their students, threatening health care workers and doctors sacrificing their lives to save lives, cheering burning masks as a gesture of freedom, I think, what's wrong with them? Don't they care about others, about life? What are they thinking/ not thinking?

I think of staged protests against Obamacare— "don't kill my grandmother" or "get government out of my Social Security and Medicare"— of people calling climate change a hoax while wildfires rage, floods destroy, drought and extreme heat make life unlivable, declaring protecting earth "elite,""too costly." Or crowds proclaiming the election stolen despite no evidence of any fraud,

What repeated soundbites made people believe lies? And who are the powerful "hit men" spreading those lies, shaping human beings who no longer care for others and are unable to see reality?

September 2nd, 2021
Let's be selfish for everyone

We're shaped by culture—family, churches, school, media, leaders. During my 30 years of teaching, I would always ask students to look closely, question, understand cause and effect, analyze, not just state opinions.

Critical thinking seems almost absent in the now "culture" shaped by narcissism, hatred, ignorance. People tearing masks from teachers, threatening health care workers, pastors calling vaccinations "demonic," governors refusing public health care mandates, DeSantis blaming Biden for COVID. Health care workers are overwhelmed, hospitals are filled by unvaccinated, and enraged "protesters" call for "freedom," describing protective measures as "tyranny." The Republican leadership and Stefanik spread toxic misinformation.

This narcissistic focus, blaming and threatening others, showing no empathy or care is a pervasive psychological sickness modeled by Trump and our Stefanik. The Dalai Lama distinguishes "foolish selfish"(pursuing only our own interests) from "wise selfish"—recognizing that our own interest lies in the welfare of everyone ... because it does.

It is essential for democracy and for our own lives to think, care, look closely, understand cause and effect, interconnections and interdependence. To practice "wise selfishness" for the good of all.

September 19th, 2021
We must save what is precious

Not the Taliban, but a growing vendetta against women: right-wing religious fundamentalists using "right to life" to restrict not just abortion but even contraception, in Texas giving citizens a bounty to report anyone assisting women in any way. .

We haven't yet lost democracy, but it's being attacked: Trump threatening election officials to change results, inspiring loyal followers to storm the Capitol, whining the election stolen; Republicans (and our Stefanik) still spouting the big lie; Republican states frantically passing laws restricting voting, firing impartial election representatives, gerrymandering, empowering state legislatures to decide election results. In 2006 Congress renewed the Voting Rights Act 98-0, but something terrible has happened to the Republican Party. Dissenting voices are threatened and McConnell insists Republicans vote against a bill to "Protect the Vote." Their people spur violent attacks against those wearing masks, against doctors, nurses, teachers. Hospitals are overwhelmed. 97% of COVID deaths are the unvaccinated.

Some wealthy people are addicted to greed; some fearful people fight to preserve white male power; some women honestly feel abortion wrong. But most people, I believe, are generous, caring, kind. How could they not see danger: the terrorist attack at the Capitol; violence in school board meetings; the insanity of DeSantis and Abbott raging against masks, vaccines, abortion while their states are ravaged by COVID, climate catastrophes, suffering. How not see the co-opting of "pro life" by hypocritical Republicans caring only for power, working against what really supports life. How not see destruction of our earth: record heat, wildfires, floods, catastrophic storms, drought, deforestation, loss of homes, lives, beauty?

We must save what's precious. If we believe in democracy: we must protect everyone's right to vote. If we value women: they must have control over their bodies. If we want our earth to flourish, we must cut fossil fuels, choose sustainable energy, fight for life.

September 30th, 2021
Let's not be ignorant about the election

Emma Goldman said, "The greatest form of violence is ignorance"—

Before and after the election, Trump spoke of election fraud, said he won the elections, filed 60 court actions, demanded audit after audit — all confirming the 2020 elections fair, free of fraud.

On Jan. 6, Trump urged followers to storm the Capitol, declaring the election stolen. He threatened election officials, called the Georgia Secretary of State Brad Raffensberger to change the state's voting totals, tried to get Vice President Pence to overturn the election.

Steven Bannon said, "Kill the Biden presidency in the crib." Flynn said the U.S. should have a coup like in Myanmar, that "it should happen here." We know that Trump had discussions with Republicans in Congress at the time of the terrorist attack.

We know that John Eastman, lawyer and adviser to Trump, outlined plans to overturn election results and install Trump as leader and that staff members of Republican attorney generals met in Atlanta to plot what to do if Trump were not elected, urging people to march to the Capitol "to stop the steal."

The 2022 Conservative Political Action Conference will be held in Hungary, where Orban, the president, has been dismantling democracy. The right wing has taken over the Republican Party, our Stefanik in the lead, repeating the lie "the election was stolen;" Republican lawmakers in 18 states have passed more than 30 laws limiting and suppressing votes.

Election workers have been threatened, dissenters on all levels harassed, those with integrity silenced. How could one be ignorant about this threat to democracy?

This has nothing to do with partisan politics, political opinions or ideology. It's what someone said (in their words) and did (in their actions) and about why some didn't want a bipartisan investigation that would reveal what is true.

October 23rd, 2021
Thoughts on the state of our union

Our Democracy is threatened, Republican state legislatures deliberately passing laws suppressing voting. Our earth is threatened with human-caused climate change: devastating hurricanes, flooding, wildfires, drought, extreme heat, air pollution. Instead of fighting against real dangers, people fight nurses, teachers, school board members as if wearing masks and getting vaccinated are affronts to freedom, as if learning a complex history, critical thinking, creative imagination are not vital to education. Yeats writes: "the worst are full of passionate intensity"—intensity for wrong causes, people stirred to actions they would never conceive themselves doing.

The now Republican Party has cast out and threatened moderates with integrity, demanding total obedience to Trump, a leader obsessed with power, parroting his dangerous lie "election was stolen," sanctioning acts of violence at the Capitol on Jan. 6, refusing bipartisan investigations, not condemning white supremacy and violence—Biden and Harris' bus pushed off the road, arsonists setting fire to Austin's Democratic office, racism, anti-Semiitism. Our homegrown brownshirts, internal terrorists, our Stec and Stefanik complicit, repeating Trump's lie, obsessively repeating "left wing socialists destroying our country."

I keep thinking surely some Republicans would support the Protect the Vote. Years ago, John Lewis' voting rights act passed 98-0. Surely some would support provisions benefiting people in their state. Biden's "Build back Better" provides what all advanced democracies already provide: Medicare expansion to cover dental, vision, extension of child tax credit, universal pre-K, family leave, subsidized child care, negotiation of drug prices, building a green economy, increasing manufacturing, training workers, good jobs. To pay for life-giving programs, he proposes raising taxes only on the wealthiest 1 percent, increasing corporate tax rate to 28%. Our economic disparity in our country is dangerous to democracy.

McConnell's made clear his "mission": blocking all legislation threatening corporate interests. Follow the money influencing the votes: fossil fuels, pharmaceuticals, banking, weapons.

November 7th, 2021
Hold accountable those who harm

Sometimes fossil fuel companies are forced to pay for damages they cause: for oil leaks, destruction of lakes and wetlands, for drinking water made toxic. Some lawsuits go further. In San Francisco where one seawall fortifying against flooding would cost the city $5 billion, the city's attorney argues, "taxpayers shouldn't be forced to shoulder that burden alone." Big oil companies knew their products caused global damage and "deceived consumers to promote and profit off those products." Mary Wood, a climate liability author, wrote: "the fossil fuel industry has yet to pay a dime in liability for the climate danger it has caused to people across the world."

In 1981, an Exxon memo revealed their knowledge that their emitted carbon monoxide could "produce effects which will indeed be catastrophic (at least for a substantial fraction of the earth's population)." Instead of acknowledging the harm, they consciously chose to spread misinformation, to create distrust in climate science, their 1998 memo stating: "Victory will be achieved when ... average citizens understand (recognize) uncertainties in climate science." The lawsuits against them name 'the industrial culprits of this absolute global catastrophe."

The Statler Brothers, the cigarette companies ... all knew the addictive qualities of their products, all lied, willing to harm in order to increase profits. Facebook lied, knowingly endangering young people's mental health. Republican "leaders" lie about nonexistent election fraud, suppress voting rights, insure their power.

Jane Goodall speaks of our need to heal all we've harmed. "Tikkun Olam" calls us to repair damage to our world.

We need to name and hold accountable those who—for profit and power—destroy people, earth and democracy. And we need to make amends and reparations to all those who have suffered.

December 12, 2021
Democracy vs. fascism

Kyle Rittenhouse—a 15-year-old who illegally purchased an assault weapon, crossed state lines, and killed two people—is a Republican hero. Rep. Boerbert yells anti-Moslim threats, Sen. Gosar pictures himself killing AOC, Republicans send Christmas cards with their children carrying guns. Gov. DeSantis creates a private militia. He and Abbott rage against masks and vaccine mandates. Books are banned and burned. People scream at teachers, nurses. Election officials are threatened, replaced, for not changing votes from Biden to Trump. States create extreme gerrymandering, suppress voting rights, give electoral authority to legislators. Gaetz, Gosar, Greene, Jim Jordan are now Republican leaders. "Disloyal" Republicans are cast out.

Some finally quit. After 16 years, Goldberg and Hayes resign from Fox News, calling Tucker Carlson's "Patriot Purge" — about Jan. 6 insurrection — "a collection of incoherent conspiracy theory mongering, riddled with factual inaccuracies, half-truths, deceptive imagery" amplifying "the false claims and bizarre narratives" of Trump. I think: how much sacrifice of integrity, soul, before speaking truth? How much damage?

The question isn't Democrats vs. Republicans but democracy vs. fascism.The American Rescue Plan and Infrastructure Bill, which Stefanik and most Republicans voted against, provided monies to states for education, police, firemen, housing, roads, bridges, broadband, mass transportation, water pipes, septic systems. Unemployment is the lowest since 1969, wages are rising, our economy growing. The Build Back Better would continue the growth: universal prekindergarten, workforce training, funding for child care, family leave, reducing pharmaceutical costs, cutting carbon, methane, shifting to renewable energies, building a livable earth for our children.

We can choose. Willful ignorance, misinformation, hatred and violence against "the other" and autocratic rule or we can choose democracy–a government serving people, recognizing the dignity and value of all beings, our interdependence and inter connection to each other and to the earth. "Peace on Earth" and "Good Will to All."

December 24th, 2021
Let goodness prevail in world

Invasive species and toxins spread easily: Emerald green bore infecting black ash, woolly adelgid infecting hemlock–healthy trees devastated. COVID spreading illness. I think of less identified pervasive toxins spread by lies–about COVID, global warming, about a "stolen election" despite overwhelming evidence of no fraud. I think of delusion–a toxin spreading in our country–"delusional disorder" characterized by irrational beliefs which a person believes to be true, so fixed that nothing, including contrary evidence, can convince a person that what they think is not true.

But if harmful toxins spread, so can goodness. When tragedy occurs, neighbors help each other. Rescue squads, nurses.   I am inspired by those risking their lives protecting our earth, fighting for democracy against despotic rulers, by whistleblowers revealing corruption. Their goodness "infects" me with hope and it, too, can spread..

During WW II, LeChambon, a small village in Southern France led by their pacifist minister refused to collaborate with Nazis. 5,000 peasants saved 5,000 Jews — gave shelter, forged papers. Hallie's "Lest Innocent Blood Be Shed" tells "how goodness happened." Camus, living in Le Chambon, wrote "The Plague,' his main character, Dr. Rieux, does all he can to heal people overwhelmed and dying of the terrible plague. He writes, "When you see the suffering it brings, you have to be mad, blind, or a coward to resign yourself to the plague." Camus' ends his novel with "the plague bacillus never dies or banishes entirely — it can remain dormant … it waits patiently."

The message: we need to be vigilant, must resist evil, do our good work to save life, to save what is precious.

In thirty years teaching—older women returning to college who were told they were stupid, prisoners told they were evil—I continually witnessed goodness spreading, each student encouraging, supporting each other, listening deeply to themselves and others, growing in understanding, consciousness, compassion. I watched goodness prevail.

January 4th, 2022
I am thinking of Jesus at this time

During this season, I have been thinking of Jesus — his history, his words, his lessons. What we know—and this is not fake news—is that Mary and Joseph were poor, looking for simple shelter (as many refugees are now). That he was born and lived as a Jew. He was a good, honest man, seeing clearly the corruption of those in power, fighting for social justice, speaking the words of the prophet Isaiah about feeding the hungry, clothing the poor. He, and prophets of the Hebrew Bible, spoke continually about compassion, welcoming the stranger, doing unto others as you would have them do unto you. Jesus was called the "prince of peace," questioning why nations rage against nation. Isaiah spoke of "beating our swords into plowshares." In our modern vocabulary, Jesus was a courageous fighter for justice, a "revolutionary" rebelling against unjust powers. With hundreds of Jews of his time and like thousands of courageous people throughout history he fought for the poor and was condemned to death by those in power.

Jesus spoke of those casting the first stone, judging others, our not seeing our own transgressions, not recognizing that we humans are not perfect, our challenge to learn from our failures and grow into our deeper more conscious selves. He spoke about turning the other cheek, about forgiveness, compassion. And over and over he preached and showed love, love for all beings. Which is why it is so strange to see so many who worship him as their savior not able to follow his most precious and timeless teachings. I wonder what he would feel today, returning to Earth, witnessing greed, corruption, hatred, violence and the worship of false prophets.

January 22nd, 2022
Lies will harm, knowledge is key

My education was a continual expansion of mind and heart. Many times I would think "I never knew that," my world continually enriched by what I hadn't known—about history, literature, science, psychology—my understanding deepening. If that made me "uncomfortable," it was because I was growing—like a teenager grows, like we all grow or should grow throughout life.

Within family, culture, religion, we're taught what to believe, often not questioning those in authority. I was an English major, reading "great" literature. The problem was that many writers were excluded from the literary "canon" — women, people of color, working class and poor people, Native Americans, immigrants — their voices, experiences, all absent. Those in authority claimed that "inclusion" would lessen "excellence," as if exclusion and excellence were the same, as if they were the only ones qualified to judge.

Fundamentalism, fascism, patriarchal power, corporate power—they were and still are, in many cases, the "masters" defining reality, writing their history—not revealing U.S. secret involvement abroad, supporting dictators to protect our corporate interests, allowing our corporate exploitation. Silencing ideas, censoring truths, banning books that threatened their power.

Anyone can demonize someone or a group, invent "facts," endlessly repeat lies, stir hatred and violence. If those people have power, their words have power over us. I think of the importance of questioning, looking closely—at the world outside of us and the world within.

Those in power will try to keep power: fossil fuel companies denying global warming; tobacco, Big Pharma all claiming their products harmless; the big lie that Trump won, the election stolen, and Jan. 6 not a violent insurrection. All intentional lies.

Who should we believe? What did we all actually see on Jan. 6? What do we actually experience: wildfires, floods, drought, glaciers melting, global warming. What do we truly value?

Follow the money, follow its power.

Lies harm. Knowledge empowers us, enabling us to choose our lives.

March 17th, 2022
On the power of misinformation

When I hear Putin naming all reality "fake news," silencing journalists who call military aggression "war," sentencing truth-tellers to prison, arresting protesters, accusing Ukrainians of doing exactly what Russian military power is doing—invading, killing innocent people, threatening chemical warfare—I think how propaganda silencing truth actually "works."

Desperate people in Ukraine calling parents in Russia hear their parents parrot Russia's fake news, not believing their own children despite cries, pleas, photographs of terrible destruction. I think: how could you not believe your children? And I think: how could we not think of parallels here, not as dire but following the same script of disinformation used by those wanting power?

In every battleground state, Republicans continually proclaim Trump won, the election stolen, I am horrified at their violent threats against those daring to speak reality.

A Russian government agency told outlets to use the words of Tucker Carlson, who sharply criticizes the actions of the U.S and NATO, blaming our country for unleashing the conflict in Ukraine.

Who are our dangerous voices spreading disinformation, suppressing truth, rousing violence?

March 26th, 2022
We need climate action right now

Sarah Bloom Raskin, nominated by Biden to be the Federal Reserve's top banking expert, was disqualified by Republicans because she actually thought that climate change — extreme weather and climate events—posed economic risks and that banks should play a role in our necessary shift from fossil fuels to clean energy.

Dr. Leach, in a recent "opinion" piece in our Post-Star, quoted Antonio Guterres, the U.N.'s secretary-general: "Today's IPCC report was an atlas of human suffering and a damning indictment of failed climate leadership. With fact upon fact, this report reveals how people and the planet are getting clobbered by climate change." Fires, floods, tornadoes, hurricanes, record heat, severe drought … climate refugees …

Yet Trump pulled us out of the Paris Climate Agreement, our country, the second largest emitter, the only one of 200 to walk away from promises to reduce green house gasses. Our Stefanik and Republicans block all legislation limiting fossil fuels and transitioning to green energy, this "pro-life" party calling it "too costly" to protect life on Earth or to make our lives more livable.

Every Saturday a few of us stand on the South Glens Falls bridge carrying a banner: "Climate Actions Now." I'm there, waving my Earth flag in the wind, feeling love for my home, pledging allegiance to our Earth and all the life that it sustains.

Earth Day 2020

April 10th, 2022
They are against what protects life

Autocratic arrogant leaders—Putin, Trump, Orban—repeat the same script: factual and accurate news is "fake news," fair elections are "rigged," violence against protesters are "law and order." All not swearing allegiance to them are socialists, communists, extreme left wing, pedophiles. Books are banned, teaching history limited, truthful people threatened. Republican state legislatures pass bills suppressing voting rights and women's reproductive rights, encouraging people to spy, sue, inform on women wanting control over their own bodies.

The Republican "culture wars" rouse hatred against false "enemies": immigrants, people of color, LGBTQ, trans people wanting to just live their lives. Sex education isn't taught in grade school, critical race theory not taught in high school –as if knowledge is dangerous..

There are real enemies, real dangers: people sickened from pollution, toxic water; devastation caused by tornadoes, floods, droughts; hurricanes intensified by climate change; earth endangered. These "pro-life" hypocrites work against what actually protects life: limiting fossil fuel emissions, creating resilient communities. Instead of "Saving Our Children," they oppose preschool education, subsidizing child care, affordable health care, lowering prescription drug costs, paid family leave, expanding Medicaid, sensible gun legislation.

Scott (R-FL) produced the current Republican "11 Point Plan to Rescue America": raising taxes on people earning less than $100,000 and ending Social Security, Medicare, Medicaid and the Affordable Care Act. Democrats have not moved left; Republicans have moved to the extreme right, their greed and will to power endangering rather than rescuing our democracy.

I think of our YMCA's core values: honesty, respect, responsibility, care. The Republican plan "to rescue America" has none of those values.

April 21st, 2022
Vote for those working for Earth

The first Earth Day was April 22, 1970. Begun in the U.S., it's now celebrated by 1 billion people around the world: to celebrate, protect, preserve our bountiful, resilient, biodiverse home. There's no Planet B.

Four local women, North Country Earth Action, urge speaking out and acting for our Earth. We can alter our personal lifestyle with less waste, less consumerism, more sustainable actions. In honor of "the global 10 days of Earth Day actions" (starting on Earth Day and ending May 1, 2022), we commit to the following. Join us whenever you can.

1. April 22: Join NY residents in Albany for an Earth Day action hosted by "Climate Can't Wait." A package of climate bills will be highlighted which we urge state legislators to pass in the 2022 legislative session. (Contact: earthactionsquad@gmail.com to carpool, meeting 10 a.m. at Exit 18 carpark.)

2. April 23: Meet NCEA at Farmers Market (Aviation Mall, 10-11 a.m) — supporting local farmers, sustainably produced products.

3. April 24: A day of personal acts of conscience: fasting; zero waste; divesting from fossil fuel investments; gardening/planting to attract pollinators … .

4. April 25: Join NCEA Light Brigade, 7:15 p.m., Crandall Public Library.

5. April 26: Zero fossil fuel day — no driving, no plastics. Recycle, compost, walk, bike.

6. April 27: No more stuff. No shopping. Repair. Reuse.

7. April 28: Eat vegetables, plant-based/free-range/grass-fed.

8. April 29: Stand with us: South Glens Falls Bridge, noon, climate action.

9. April 30: Pop up: Divest action, portable climate clock. City Park, 10-11 a.m.

10. May 1: Public service day. Donate to food pantries, reuse centers; clean waterways, parks; write letters to newspapers.

And always be conscious of what we buy: paper towels, toilet paper, cosmetics, textiles, foods, pesticides ... where they come from and the "cost" to our environment and to workers.

Vote for those working for protection and preservation of our Earth.

May 12th, 2022
GOP voices used to be thoughtful

It's hard to understand how kind, good people become loyal followers of someone arrogant, threatening, demanding total power, caring only for himself.

What has his Republican Party given us? The very wealthy had their taxes greatly lowered, regulations restraining drilling, mining, pollution of air and water struck down. International relationships with democracies were severed, environmental commitments to prevent climate crisis dismissed. Climate change, COVID were labeled "hoaxes," the committee investigating the violent attack on our Capitol and democracy was called a partisan witch hunt. Most Republicans were pressured to declare our fair election was "stolen." Republican legislatures rushed to pass hundreds of laws gerrymandering districts, suppressing voting rights, banning women's reproductive rights.

In the past, there were thoughtful Republican voices. President Eisenhower warned against the power of the military industrial complex, spoke of our right to join unions, the necessity of preserving Social Security, unemployment insurance and said, "If a political party does not have in its foundation the determination to advance a cause that is just and moral, it is not a political party; it is merely a conspiracy to seize power" and if it "values privileges above its principles it soon loses both." President Nixon created the EPA, the Clean Air Act, Safe Drinking Water Act, Endangered Species Act. Bipartisan legislation protected our Earth.

How did the now Republican Party lose its ethical center, swearing allegiance to a fascist dictator? I pledge allegiance to our earth: "one planet in our care, irreplaceable, with sustenance and respect for all" and to our democracy "with liberty and justice for all."

June 9th, 2022
The relinquishing of integrity, caring

There was a time when Republicans supported environmental legislation, voted for the voting rights act, supported sensible gun control, were caring, thoughtful. Even the NRA supported gun safety, background checks.

There was a time when Stefanik was moderate.

Bridgeland wrote of securing Stefanik a position in Bush's administration, viewing her as "a bright light, focused on problem solving … having character." But something happened. When Stefanik became a strong MAGA supporter of the "stolen election" lie, spouting white supremacist "great replacement theory," Bridgeland was "shocked Stefanik would go down such a dark path": "No power, no position, is worth the complete loss of your integrity. It was alarming to me to watch this transformation. … She wanted to climb Republican ranks and she's climbed the ladder on the back of lies about the election that undermine trust in elections, putting people's lives at risk."

What happened to her is what has happened to the Republican Party: loss of integrity, conspiracy theories, attacking everything that is precious: justice, freedom, equality, democracy.. Their adopted "agenda": religious extremism; laws controlling women's bodies; voter suppression; stirring fear of immigrants, gays, trans, Jews, people of color; rousing domestic terrorism. We have suffered over 200 mass shootings this year. The Republicans' response: more guns.

June 25th, 2022
Both encouraged and dismayed

I often call the offices of the small remnant of Republican lawmakers who are not believing conspiracy theories, not posing with guns, not yelling "pedophiles" and "RINO" at anyone dissenting from the big lie, not rousing their base to violence, not seeing violence and hatred as "normal." I call just to thank them for having some integrity, speaking truth, voting for what is good.

I thank those who voted for the infra-structure bill, or sensible gun control, who recognized that Biden actually won the election, who voted for impeachment, thank all who were attacked by Trump, cast out by Republican "leaders." And I am moved when I hear conservative Republicans, those who supported and voted for Trump, his own lawyers, advisers, campaign chairs, legislators, clerks, speak the truth about events, saying they would not break their own oath to our constitution despite pressure and even threats.

We learn how everyone around Trump told him that there was no evidence the election was rigged, how he persisted, intentionally lying. How Pence's clerks feared for him, the crowd, prompted by Trump, yelling "hang Pence." How Judge Luttig, a leading conservative judge, warned that Jan. 6 "was a war for America's democracy, a war irresponsibly instigated and prosecuted by the former president, his political allies, and his supporters ... putting America itself at stake."

I heard Arizona's state legislature's Rusty Bowers, Georgia's Secretary of State Raffensberger, and deputy Sterling speak about Trump's unrelenting pressure to change votes, declare the election fraudulent, support false slates of electors. I was moved–sometimes to tears– by their courage and integrity, their keeping their oath to the Constitution, God and democracy, they and their family harassed, threatened, and attacked. Heard Ruby Freeman, a Georgia election worker, and her mother threatened and traumatized by angry mobs for being faithful election workers proud of doing good work.

I am always moved by integrity and courage in the face of threats. And I am dismayed by people like Representative Stefanik, sacrificing integrity and soul for power.

July 7th, 2022
'Pro-life' focus is endangering our democracy

When I hear some "pro-life" women opposing women's reproductive rights, I can feel their honest passion, recognize it as my own passion for life, for preserving Earth and all living beings, for civil rights and climate justice, for legislation promoting voting, promoting democracy. But when I hear the mostly men Republican legislators in many states ranting about "life, I hear lawmakers who care nothing about children, women, or woman's rights. I see Republican legislators passing countless laws against women's control over their bodies—vigilantes spying, laws imprisoning women for crossing state lines, providers prosecuted for felonies, people fearful. I see Republican legislators refusing to expand Medicaid in states with the highest infant and maternal mortality and the most executions. I see states that have almost no gun regulation and take away the ability of the federal government's EPA to enact restrictions on carbon emissions and toxins which cause harm, states and legislators not concerned at all with "life."

Clarence Thomas has put gay marriage and even contraception on the potential chopping block, Thomas whose wife attended the Jan. 6 insurrection and tried to convince states to change their electoral votes.

They are not pro-life but forces of control and power.

July 21st, 2022
Commenting on the 'extreme right wing' in America

People believe dangerous lies, lies intentionally spread for power, lies believed in ignorance: the shootings in Newtown, Parkland, Uvalde were "staged"; Russia invaded to "save" Ukrainians; fossil fuels don't contribute to climate crisis; 2020's fair election was "stolen"; whites are superior to Blacks, men superior to women.

Meteorologists now name climate change as a leading cause for the devastation we witness: extreme killing heat, severe droughts, disastrous wildfires, flooding, glaciers melting, oceans warming, acidifying, massive extinctions, climate refugees. They say what Fox News, the fossil fuel industry and paid politicians deny–that our earth is in crisis and we must reduce emissions, stop drilling, deforestation, soil depletion. We must shift to sustainable energies to save our home, our planet earth.

Life on Earth is threatened. Yet Republicans veto any legislation that Biden proposes to lessen fossil fuels, build green infrastructure with American workers, mitigate and adapt to future climate disasters. Democracy is threatened, yet Republicans and our Supreme Court undercut voting rights, wage a vendetta against women, support Trump's lies.

The question: how to fight against ignorance and for earth and democracy.

August 7th, 2022
Some sunshine filters in among the gloom

In Kansas, it was a victory for women's reproductive rights — the vote 60% to 40% in a very conservative state. But it was more than that. It was independent people refusing to allow fundamentalist religion, right-wing Republican legislatures, an extreme ideological Supreme Court, and bullies threatening and using their power to control our lives.

The majority of people do not want the overturning of Roe v. Wade, want EPA to regulate toxins in air and water, want to raise the minimum wage, want lower prescription drug costs and Medicare to negotiate prices; want to ban military-style assault weapons and raise the age for purchase to 21; want child tax credit and paid family leave, good public education; want the wealthy to pay their fair share of taxes. They want a sustainable and resilient Earth for their children.

How was this extreme right-wing minority able to enforce their will on the majority? Through a red state strategy and gerrymandering which gave them Republican controlled legislatures, through misinformation and repeated lies, through fabricated and manipulated fear of 'the "communist left wing Democrats," through fear of an "invasion' by immigrants, by Blacks and Jews, of losing their "privilege" as man, or as a white person, or as a heterosexual or Christian…Through fear of living in a democratic and diverse society with all peoples having equal rights.

August 25th, 2022
What side are we on

On one side are people doing work that heals, that nourishes life. In government, we see legislation helping communities: the American Rescue Plan (funding schools, firemen, police, businesses …); Infrastructure Bill (bridges, septic and water, broadband); CHIP (subsidizing manufacturing of semi-conductors, good jobs here); PACK (medical treatment for veterans suffering from toxic burn pits); the Inflation Reduction Bill (lowering prescription drug costs, extending health care subsidies, reducing carbon emissions through consumer and manufacturing incentives and tax credit for clean energy). A 15% minimum tax on corporations earning more than one billion in annual profits. And continual attempts to pass child tax credit, subsidized child care, free preschool, family leave, affordable housing. And, always, empathy, care, assistance for those suffering environmental devastation (Kentucky) and mass shootings (Uvalde, Highland).

On the other side: the "signature" Republican tax bill (2017) slashing corporate taxes, adding 2 trillion to our deficit; Trump removing regulations protecting air and water and withdrawing from international climate agreements and from NATO allies. We see a vendetta against women and their reproductive rights, an allegiance to the NRA, voter suppression legislation, ridiculous conspiracy theories. We get programs undercutting public schools, Social Security, Medicare. And we hear Trump endlessly repeating the lie that the election was stolen, endorsing only those swearing allegiance to him, threatening dissenters, rousing violence and hatred at the Capitol, ranting against the FBI, election workers, legislators, anyone speaking truth. Endangering democracy, praising autocrats.

The Republican Lincoln Brigade chronicles the end of the GOP: "What remains shares the name and branding of the traditional Republican Party, but is in fact an authoritarian nationalist cult dedicated only to Donald Trump." Luce, in the conservative Financial Times, writes: "I've covered extremism and violent ideologies around the world. Have never come across a political force more nihilistic, dangerous and contemptible than today's Republicans."

The question for all of us: What side are we on?

September 13th, 2022
Vote: integrity, caring and a livable Earth

Biden named what leaders of democratic countries, journalists, historians, and thoughtful people see and fear — the danger of Maga Republicans, the threat of fascism. The signs: refusal to recognize fair free elections; voter suppression; unqualified candidates swearing loyalty to a dangerous dictator; violence against targeted "enemies," religion and government intertwined in Christian nationalism; disdain for intellectual thought, art; labeling news "fake," elections "rigged"; idealizing "masculinity," parading with guns, demeaning women; protecting corporate power; undercutting public education, Social Security, Medicare.

Republicans claim support for "law and order" but are silent when their base terrorizes poll workers, governors, and Republicans speaking the truth under oath, silent when violent insurrectionists attack Capitol police. Instead of condemning Trump's stealing top security classified documents, they attack the FBI, Department of Justice. Trump warns "there will be violence in the streets," vows to pardon insurrectionists and, if elected, to imprison those who are against him, using the" insurrection act" to call the military against any protestors. He promises o use the law to impose his will and power..

How could people vote for him? I am dismayed and horrified....

October 9th, 2022
'Immoral people in power'

In Iran thousands are protesting not just the police killing of a Kurdish woman but the "morality police" enforcing rigid fundamentalist "morality" on women and society. In the U.S., we have our own "morality police" — an extreme right-wing religious and political minority imposing their will: telling teachers what they can teach, telling students what they can learn, censoring and banning books, controlling women's reproductive choices, restricting voting, rousing fear against immigrants "invading" and violence against gays, trans, Blacks, Jews just living their lives.

Republicans campaign on Democrats being "soft on crime," on their "backing the blue." I back the blue — the Capitol Police courageously protecting our Capitol, our local police protecting our community, the Department of Justice enforcing just laws — but not police storming the Capitol or beating workers protesting conditions, or Blacks attempting to vote. It's important to question slogans, examine words, look at actions.

The Republican Party speaks of "law and order" but is silent when their "base" commits acts of violence, when Trump demands obedience, threatens dissenters, claims the fair election "stolen." Fearing his autocratic wrath, most in his party echo his lies, casting out honest Republicans who have integrity. Trump endorses unqualified, hypocritical politicians whose only "virtue' is devotion to him, repeating lies and spouting slogans and Biblical quotes (Herschel Walker one of many). Stefanik becomes a MAGA "leader," objecting to election certification after the Capitol violence, voting against the "Election Reform Act," silent about Trump's attempt to overthrow democracy. Denouncing "extreme left wing socialists," she blames Biden for everything, voting against but taking credit for Biden's legislation helping and enriching our community and mitigating our climate crisis.

Stefanik and 299 Republican candidates are election deniers, many believing absurd conspiracy theories. If they win, we lose: integrity, justice, democracy, a livable earth.

To think of these immoral people in power is frightening and keeps me awake at night. To think of my neighbors cheering him, voting for him, is heartsickening.

October 22nd, 2022
Many questions.

By what incredible trickery have the Republicans managed to make truth a "partisan witch hunt" and make what is false true? How is it possible that the Republicans have made Trump's totally false claim of a "stolen election" believable? How can they make Trump's big lie a criteria for his endorsement of unqualified candidates, and how could people vote for them? How do they convince people that a violent insurrection was a peaceful protest and that those storming the Capitol are heroes worthy of pardon? How could "religious" evangelicals see Trump, a corrupt and arrogant demagogue, as "prophet," "savior"? How could Stefanik take credit for all she voted against? And how could people think Biden and Democrats are dangerous demons, left-wing socialists who have destroyed our country when they passed legislation benefiting our communities: child tax credit, family leave, lower drug prices, free preschool, affordable housing, infrastructure, broadband, incentivizing green energies, bringing manufacturing jobs to the U.S., raising taxes on the extremely wealthy? And why would they think that our economy–with low unemployment, increased wages, unions growing in power– is terrible? And how could anyone think Republicans could solve inflation when their "signature tax bill" lowered taxes on those very wealthy, creating a huge deficit? When they helped manufacturers move factories abroad, and when they would, if they could, privatize Social Security and Medicare?

And how could they convince people that "Democrats are soft on crime" when Republicans are complicit in covering up the attempt to overthrow the will of the people, when they are silent about white supremacy and domestic violence, when they attack women's right to control their own body, when the most violence is in states with the most guns and the most lax gun laws?.

How could people believe absurd conspiracy theories...not see what is obvious...not question? If it is a cultural war, what is the culture they want to enforce?

November 17th, 2022
How could we not see what's obvious?

UN Secretary General Guterres told delegates at COP27 "We are in the fight of our lives, and we are losing. The clock is ticking. … Greenhouse gas emissions keep growing, global temperatures keep rising, and our planet is fast approaching the tipping point that will make climate chaos irreversible. We are on a highway to climate hell with our foot still on the accelerator." ... "Human activity is the cause of the climate problem, so human action must be the solution."

How could we not see what's obvious? Drought, floods, killing heat, wildfires, melting glaciers, polluted air and water, loss of biodiversity, of life. How could we not care about the world our children will inherit? How could we not do everything to save our home?

November 27, 2022
Protecting what is precious

There are so many here, around the world, and throughout history doing "good"—acts to protect sacred land, endangered species, our oceans, rivers, drinking water, air; to stop deforestation, drilling and mining of fossil fuels. Courageous people protesting dictators and repressive regimes in Hong Kong, Belarus, Myanmar, Iran, Syria; journalists protecting free speech in Philippines, Mexico; lawyers and religious leaders protecting separation of church and state; and our neighbors working in food pantries and homeless shelters, welcoming immigrants. ... People doing good work.

But others do great harm—for power and greed, in hatred and ignorance.

The poet Unamuno said to Franco's generals, "You will win because you have brute force but to persuade you'd need what you lack—right and reason for Spain's very soul"; Victor Jara, the Chilean guitarist, kept singing while being shot by Pinochet's police. I hear their words with voices of survivors of gun violence in Parkland, churches, synagogues, Colorado's gay bar, along with thousands of courageous people imprisoned—all proclaiming the power of right and reason, the power love, the reality that "we are family."

On my desk I have a card:"You thought you buried us; you didn't know we were seeds."

This Thanksgiving I thank all the seeds patiently waiting to sprout, the hard work, resistance, and struggle of so many to encourage and foster those seeds, and all those who have cultivated, cared for, and protected what is precious.

December 24th, 2022
Two lessons for this holiday season

How do we expand a story—a specific narrative in a specific time—to its deeper and larger "message"?

During Christmas, I think of the story of Joseph, a poor carpenter, and Mary, pregnant, looking for shelter, giving birth to the baby Jesus in a stable, a poor Jewish family needing a safe home. I think of Jesus' life, his healing powers, love and compassion, his blessing the poor, a revolutionary working for justice and against greed and hypocrisy. And because people believed in his message and followed him, the Roman power elite sought to silence him, punish him and all dissenters, hanging him on the cross, the traditional punishment for those who questioned those in power. .

The simple and deep message for me: to welcome the stranger; to clothe, feed and give shelter to the poor and hungry; to protest against unjust power; to recognize and the goodness of those who give their lives to create a more just world.

A deep message for all time.

January 12th, 2023
GOP agenda does not reflect Americans' priorities

Republicans in Congress say they will do what people elected them to do. But does the public really want lowering taxes on the wealthy, removing regulations protecting our environment, not dealing with the climate crisis, increasing defense spending, limiting curriculum and spending in public schools, weakening Social Security and Medicare, repealing the capping of drug prices? Republicans promise investigating Hunter Biden, Joe Biden, and the Jan. 6 committee, but not the perpetrators of the violence at the Capitol or those who roused that violence. For many, compromise is "betrayal." Moderate Republicans—voting in a bipartisan way for their communities—have been cast out.

U.S. Rep. Jamie Raskin, D-Maryland, said "our system cannot be a system of justice where foot soldiers go to jail but the masterminds and ringleaders get a free pass." Many now sitting in Congress are the "masterminds"— election deniers, supporters of the insurrection, working to suppress voting rights.

I'd like to believe that most Amsericans have common needs and values: clean air and drinking water, regulations protecting us from toxins and gun violence, safe and affordable homes, livable wages, affordable medical care, good public education, subsidized child care and child tax credits, family leave for illnesses, good bridges, roads. I believe most want an immigration policy that protects our borders but recognizes that people coming to our country are people fleeing violence, poverty, arid land where they can no longer farm, that most feel our country's responsibility to  welcome those seeking legal asylum, feel that immigrants can enrich our country, become needed workers on our farms and factories, revive our schools and our community. And I would hope that we all remember on some deep level that we, too, were refugees, immigrants looking for a home.

I would like to believe that most Americans value fairness, justice, care, kindness, integrity, respect—not bullying or violence, not an arrogance that assumes one person or group superior to another, that we all want thoughtful debates about real issues and real solutions, not revenge, blame, hatred, violence.

I would like to believe that what I believe is still true in America.

January 24th, 2023
Act with integrity for what is moral, just

It's healthy to debate values, beliefs, ideas, to question, learn, grow, and, even, feel discomfort when old beliefs no longer feel true. What isn't good is to threaten, silence, rouse fear and hatred — to intentionally lie. Trump and his supporters intentionally lied, called the election rigged, spouted ridiculous conspiracy theories, attempted to change election results, roused violence, called insurrection a "peaceful protest." Election deniers, complicit in undercutting democracy, sit in the House of Representatives: Greene, Gosar, Boerbert, Perry now heading the previously bipartisan Oversight Committee. The fox "guarding" the chicken house.

Big Lies have always existed, perpetuated by those in power. I remember learning about CIA involvement overthrowing democratically elected leaders: Mosaddegh (Iran), Allende (Chile), Arbenz (Guatemala), our government supporting military dictators and corrupt leaders in El Salvador, Argentina, Bolivia, Honduras. Reading investigative reporting, I saw how tobacco, Enron and fossil fuels, Big Pharma, chemical companies continually lied about the harm caused by their products.

There are lies so pervasive people believe them true — the "superiority" of whites, males, Europeans, humans– believing the "morality" and even goodness of imperialism, colonialism, genocide of Native peoples, slavery, misogyny, exploitation of Earth. Taliban forbidding girls to be educated, women to work; religious fundamentalists, Iran and here, suppressing women's autonomy; dictators using military violence against those wanting freedom, imprisoning, torturing, executing. And we, in human arrogance, abusing animals and our Earth, as if Earth was a commodity to be exploited.

It's good to learn history, to be awake, to be "wok," to continually enlarge our vision of what was and what is, to say "now I see"--an amazing grace enabling us to act with knowledge, wisdom and integrity.

February 7th, 2023
'Masters' are blind to worth and dignity

Eichmann, the architect of the Nazi extermination of 6 million Jews, bragged of his "blood ancestry," his "master Aryan" race. I think of the strange delusion of "masters" throughout history: white slaveholders savagely beating slaves; whites in the Jim Crow South lynching Black men, passing laws forbidding blacks access to state colleges, to buying homes, to voting; men denying women the right to vote, exploiting and abusing women, creating laws forbidding women's education, work, reproductive rights; religious fundamentalists declaring homosexuality "blasphemy" punishable by death; Republican legislatures banning books, restricting courses in history, literature, sex education; self-righteous people violently attacking librarians, teachers, health care workers, sex educators in the name of parental "freedom"; Western "advanced" countries and corporate powers assuming their right to exploit and subjugate land and people. Who are these people feeling morally superior while committing immoral acts of cruelty and harm?

Throughout history those in power, those "masters," have viewed themselves as the moral center of the universe, blind to the worth, dignity, value, bounty, beauty, and life of all beings and of our Earth in its extraordinary biodiversity. And throughout history people have been died for their deeper and truer vision: Gandhi, MLK, Robert Kennedy, Rabin.

It is heart sickening to see Modi, the Hindu nationalist prime minister of India, betraying Gandhi's work for peace and unity; to see Netanyahu and Israel's now right-wing government allied with those who assassinated Rabin, now rousing Jewish racist settlers to violence in the West Bank; to have right-wing Republicans put in power election deniers, conspiracy theorists, racists; to have whistleblowers and fighters for democracy and protection of Earth labeled "terrorists."

I can see why DeSantis and many Republican legislators work to restrict what we learn, what we know, what we say, who we are ... , want us ignorant of the courage of those who resisted abusive power and fought for justice and freedom throughout our history.

March 18th, 2023
Urge banks to stop financing fossil fuels

It's immoral to consciously cause great harm for greed. What is now abundantly clear, unless we choose willful ignorance, is that intense global warming is destroying life; much of wildlife is threatened with extinction; drought and floods force people to leave homes; water is becoming scarce, hurricanes more extreme. Earth's biodiversity — the source of all life — is endangered.

Expanded and new investment in fossil fuels is not the path for progress but of death. Increasing carbon dioxide and methane destroys life. Four banks — Chase, Citibank, Wells Fargo and Bank of America — are "climate criminals," their investments accounting for one quarter of all fossil fuel financing. They are the "pipeline" and we who invest in them are complicit. Rabbi Heschel speaking about social injustice said: "We are not all guilty, but we are all responsible."

On March 21 in Albany and around our country, there is a Day of Action to Stop the Money Pipeline — a coalition of Green Faith (different religious faiths), McKibben's Third Act, trade unions declaring "if you don't move money out of fossil fuels, we will move our money out of your banks." There will be marches to the banks, people tearing up their credit cards, speeches, rocking grannies ... naming as "criminal" those choosing profit over life.

Those in power often misname the "criminals": indigenous people protecting sacred land from drilling; women helping women access health care; trans people seeking to live authentically. What is "criminal" are legislatures in Alabama, Mississippi drawing voting districts consciously limiting votes of black and poor; legislatures demanding banks not consider climate change as part of investment strategy; laws removing regulations protecting our air, water, earth from toxins, banks from fraud, trains from derailment; politicians wanting power, claiming a free, fair election "stolen." And banks investing in destruction of our earth.

It is important to name and punish criminals who do harm to life.

March 30th, 2023
Include diverse voices in studies

In undergraduate school, I studied the "canon of great literature," only later realizing it was "the masters' canon" — white men who, consciously or unconsciously, excluded women, African Americans, the poor, workers, Hispanics, immigrants, gay, lesbians — all who were "not them." When their voices were included in the "canon," critics bemoaned loss of "excellence." In her book *Transforming Knowledge*, Minnich writes: "Calls for a new inclusivity are heard as threatening excellence itself ... but what is put in question is, quite simply, exclusivity" — the power to keep others out. When those "others" were included, my world expanded in richness, depth, bounty. History too expanded, not only "his story" but stories of struggles, courage, wisdom of those not in power — indigenous peoples, slaves, women, immigrants, workers, voices of trees, animals, other sentient beings.

Recently the Vatican Archives, under lock and key from 1939-1958, were opened, Pope Francis wanting "increased transparency," declaring "the Church is not afraid of history." That transparency revealed what had been purposely hidden–Vatican's support of Nazis during and after WWII and 2,000 years of anti-Semitism. Researchers understood the importance of truth, clear evidence, "honoring victims and survivors." They wanted to understand why and how "good people throughout history become involved in cruelty and destruction"--the importance of knowing, the danger of ignorance. I wanted and still want to understand, to know.

Who are today's "masters" afraid of history? Florida Gov. Ron DeSantis' attacking academic freedom; condemning inclusion, equity, diversity; disallowing gender and African American studies, subjects encouraging children to question, think, grow. Banning books, censoring teachers, appointing conservative trustees, creating fear. Declaring "Freedom" for religious right Christians, "parental rights" for chosen parents. "Taking America Back" — backwards, into ignorance.

When Ken Burns did his PBS documentary on the United States and the Holocaust, he was asked why he did it. He said something like: "Do you see the people there, raising their hands in Nazi salute, throwing stones, killing Jews? They were like us. And we could be like them." That is my great fear. It happened then and it could happen here.

Don't we want to understand how "people throughout history become involved in cruelty"? Don't we want to learn how others showed great courage in resisting?

April 23rd, 2023
Republicans are now party of crazy

It would have been a different story if, when Trump lost in 2020, he conceded to Biden instead of spending years shouting the election "stolen," getting Fox News and majority of Republican politicians repeating the lie, rousing a mob to attack our Capitol. The Republican Party would still have passed their "signature tax bill" giving huge tax breaks to the wealthy, increasing deficit and income inequality. They would still remove regulations protecting our air, water, and earth, catering to corporate interests and fossil fuels. But they wouldn't be crazy, wouldn't court white supremacists and anti-Semites, spread absurd conspiracy theories, treat a threatening, arrogant Trump as god. They'd be for the Second Amendment but not make Kyle Rittenhouse a hero for killing two protestors or send Christmas greetings with their kids holding rifles.

Stefanik and MAGAN Republicans obsessively repeat their robotic "script" about "dangerous extreme far left Biden/Democrats, socialists (pedophiles) destroying our country." They blame Soros (i.e. Jews) for supporting Bragg and all investigations into truth. Evidence, facts, questioning are dismissed as witch hunts. Words like freedom, parental rights, and family values are used to arouse anger against teachers, election workers, librarians, climate scientists: to ban books, control curriculum, defund public libraries. Instead of legislation to support our real needs, they pass hundreds of laws against trans, against women's reproductive choices. In the name of preventing nonexistent fraud, they pass bills restricting and suppressing voting rights. Rigged gerrymandering has deprived many communities of any voice. Tennessee expelled two black Democrats for speaking out for safe gun safety. Who are these people wanting power and control?

It's important to be awake/aware/woke. Don't most people want dignity, respect; value kindness, caring, justice, fairness; want good work, livable wages, medical care, affordable housing. They want democracy, not despotic rulers, violence, want to preserve and protect our fragile and endangered earth? And if that is true, how could they vote for Trump and Stefanik?

May 4th, 2023
Minority oppresses will of the majority

    Sandy Senn, a South Carolina Republican, united with five female lawmakers in opposition to a near-total abortion ban, saying: "abortion laws, each and every one of them, have been about control, plain and simple. And in the Senate the males all have control." I felt moved by the strength of his words, his seeing so clearly the issue of control. And I felt enraged that In Tennessee's Senate, two African American legislators were expelled because of their advocacy for gun safety, the legislature passing a "permitless gun carry law," banning all speakers and, in Montana, the only trans legislator was expelled for speaking about violence against the trans community. The issue of control, of who controls whom. A question of power.

    In Afghanistan the Taliban exerts total power and control over women — limiting their education, their work, their lives. In Myanmar, Hong Kong, Belarus, hundreds of thousands of people wanting democracy are silenced, arrested, killed. Putin, Asad… poison, imprison. And here, the "Freedom Caucus," the Christian right wing, the ideological Supreme Court, and big corporations (fossil fuels, big pharma, the NRA, corporate lobbyists) use their money and power to buy politicians to do their bidding. Michigan voters voted to create impartial and fair redistricting. But 29 Republican states chose a different route: voter suppression (targeting black communities) and extreme partisan gerrymandering, giving themselves supermajorities, allowing them to legislate whatever they want, no longer feeling obligated to represent diverse people in their states, no longer allowing people to have a voice.

May 16th, 2023
Strong action needed now on climate change

To Sen. Dan Stec and Assemblyman Matt Simpson a letter from the northcountryearthaction

In 1988, James Hansen put Congress on notice that global warming was happening, and we had better do something about it quickly. Science has given us dire warnings repeatedly since then. The latest 2023 scientific report from the prestigious IPCC (Intergovernmental Panel on Climate Change) again warned of catastrophic rising global temperatures and more extreme weather events.

We listened and acted in New York. In 2019, our state Legislature, responding to the call to decrease our reliance on fossil fuels, passed the CLCPA (Climate Leadership & Community Protection Act) with innovative doable goals. A panel of experts was established to develop the "scoping plan" for CLCPA enactment with public input. The plan was finalized in December 2022. The current NY budget includes funding to enact the CLCPA as recommended by this panel of experts. No amendments. No excuses. No delays. The fossil fuel industry may prioritize profit, but we prioritize our future.

And yet, in the 4-2-2023 Post-Star article about the CLCPA, both of you, Senator Stec and Assemblyman Simpson, were interviewed and sounded hesitant to give your full support. When we face the enormity of potential harm from increased atmospheric CO_2 and methane, there is no place for hesitancy. The legislature must follow through with the climate actions as recommended, despite politics, despite corporate pressures. Harsh and harsher weather is expected due to ongoing climate warming. The CLCPA may seem costly now, but any delay will increase future costs. Enacting the CLCPA without amendments is mandatory.

And so, we ask for your full support of the CLCPA. We ask for your words to be seen in local news and heard in public statements. You speak for us. You speak for our planet.

Lisa Adamson, Catherine Atherden, Diane Collins,
founders of North Country Earth Action

May 21st, 2023
GOP is now party of guns and paranoia

Powerful Republicans repeat the same response to every mass shooting: more guns in more places, mental health counseling, prayers. Clearly more guns isn't the answer. Texas and Republican states with most guns and least gun safety laws, have the highest rates of gun violence.

They are, however, right about the need for mental health counseling, not just for those individuals killing with assault weapons but for those in power consciously promoting hate, violence, ignorance. Our culture is "sick"— delusion, addiction, greed, paranoia. The delusion that guns save rather than endanger ("compulsive behavior despite adverse consequences"); the delusion spread by Trump and MAGA Republicans that our election was stolen despite no evidence, Fox News admitting finally their deliberate disinformation. And Trump's mental illness of narcissism, defined as "arrogance, lack of empathy, preoccupation with power, exploiting others for one's own gain."

Trump and his loyal followers feel angry, fearful, aggrieved — paranoia defined as "unwarranted or delusional belief one is being persecuted, harassed betrayed." Trump obsessively declaring all careful investigation as "witch hunts. In their fear and paranoia, Republican state legislators pass hundreds of laws against those who do them no harm: trans, women wanting control over their bodies. Their own fear creates fear in teachers, doctors, librarians, children, their need for control they ban books, defunding libraries, public schools, public broadcasting.

I think of the pervasive delusion throughout history that men, whites, Christians, humans are superior, the center of the universe. The "sickness" of greed (desire for more income, possessions power, privilege), their abusing, exploiting Earth and all beings for profit. Perhaps the deepest "delusion" is that we're separate from all other beings, not connected to our extraordinary, intricate, interdependent web of life, a delusion that allows us to destroy our own precious home.

June 4th, 2023
Desire for control takes away rights

Watching the Memorial Day concert, I was moved by the honoring of those who fought for our country, who died, were imprisoned, traumatized by war and violence. There was no patriotic jargon about the glory of war — wars I often questioned — but honoring the courage of those who served and sacrificed. The focus was on our oneness as a people, a country united, something I felt when I marched in our Glens Falls Memorial Parade — school bands playing, different groups marching, I marching with my earth flag and our northcountryearthaction banner "Protect our Earth," the NAACP in front of us. A diverse group of marchers and people cheering, smiling.

So different from the violence, threats, anger that I hear and fear from individuals attacking libraries, schools, health clinics, boycotting Target and stores celebrating gay pride, different from Republican legislatures passing hundreds of laws against gays and trans, attacking women's rights, warning of dangerous refugees "invading" our country, condemning "inclusion, diversity, and equity" as if they were evil, naming art, music, critical thinking "wok."

They use names like "Moms for liberty," "Parents' rights," The Freedom Caucus … What I hear is not rights (which should be for all beings), not family or religious values (love, compassion, kindness, integrity, honesty) but desire for control and power, using threats and violence against others who are not "them," against people of other colors, identities, beliefs who want to just live their lives.

Laws, threats, violence silence people, create fear. Teachers, librarians, doctors, nurses, parents, children all leave states where they do not feel safe or welcomed, where they are unable to practice medical healing work, read books which speak to them, attend schools challenging them, where they feel demeaned by threatening bullies.

What would it mean to recognize the dignity and worth of all beings and the richness of diversity, inclusion, and equity?

July 9th, 2023
'Ranting" is concern for Earth, Democracy

I'm inspired by those risking prison and life to protect what is precious: preserving old growth forests, sacred land, endangered species; fighting for clean water, clean air, against polluters exploiting earth for greed; believing truth and justice matter. On trains: "if you see something dangerous, tell somebody"; streets: "drive/act like your children live here." I think of Daniel Ellsberg's decision to print the Pentagon papers exposing government lies about the war in Vietnam; Rabbis for human rights in Israel protecting Palestinian land, olive trees and life from violent attacks by Jewish settlers; those in Myanmar, Belarus, around the world silenced, imprisoned, tortured, killed for peacefully demanding democracy.

Those wanting total power label peaceful protestors "terrorists." MAGA Republicans — once censured for conspiracy theories, anti-Semitism, racism — are now the leaders of the party, introducing impeachment procedures against Biden, censuring Schiff, investigating the Justice Department, anyone (Republican or Democrat) daring to speak what's clearly true.

Asked why he brought to light the pentagon papers, Ellsberg answered: "who will put this information out if I don't." Schiff on the Republicans' censuring him, said: "You who are the authors of a big lie about the last election must condemn the truth — and I stand proudly before you. Your words tell me that I've been effective in defense of our democracy."

My small act in defense of democracy is writing two letters to The Post-Star every month, beginning years ago with anger at Bush/Cheney's lies claiming "weapons of mass destruction," leading us into an unprovoked war against Iraq, costing many lives. Accused of "ranting," I answer: I rant about greed destroying our earth for profit, intentional lies rousing hatred and violence. I "rant" because I love our biodiverse endangered earth, our fragile, precious democracy …because peace, justice, caring are possible. I am inspired by Jimmy Carter who said, "My faith demands that I do whatever I can, wherever I can, for as long as I can."

July 25th, 2023
GOP ignores threats to Earth, democracy

My friend in Vermont saw the flood stop a few feet from his home. How close does something have to be to see danger — to our lives, homes, children, Earth, democracy? Ken Burns spoke about his PBS program "The U.S. and the Holocaust" stressing the importance of knowing history. The program showed the build up of violence in Nazi Germany, of "good" "moral" people rounding up gypsies, gays, socialists, killing Jews who were their neighbors, cheering and saluting Hitler, their savior, Burns said, "they were people like us…and we could easily be like them."

How close does something have to be to see danger?

August 12th, 2023
Christianity should embrace love

Last month I saw "Mama Bears" on PBS, a program about very religious Christian mothers who had accepted their church's judgment of homosexuality as evil, as sin. Believing the preachers, they tried desperately to change their children. At some point, however, they began to change, some after hearing mothers speak of the suicide of beloved children– mothers speaking with deep pain, sorrow, remorse. Talking with other mothers, they began to change, started seeing their God as loving rather than wrathful, their children as unique, beautiful. Naming themselves "mama bears," they created a community of love, going to pride events, hugging everyone, cooking dinners in homeless shelters housing gay kids, attending gay weddings to celebrate couples who were cast out by their parents. They became loving mamabears, moving from hate and fear to love of God and life. They were joyous.

When I saw "Moms for Liberty" — a religious Christian group supporting laws restricting trans and gays, banning books, speaking words of hate — identify as "mamabears" I was dismayed and emailed Karrie Fletcher, one of the founders of mamabears. She wrote right back, saying, "No, we aren't affiliated with 'Moms for Liberty' at all. They are the complete opposite of who we are and what we stand for." These mama bears had redefined — as we all need to do — freedom, liberty, rights, Christianity, and love.

Right-wing evangelicalism has narrowed "Christianity" to the battle against abortion, gays and trans, against women as pastors and leaders, ignoring the deep essential teachings of Christianity, the actual words of Jesus and prophets of all religions: love they neighbor, welcome the stranger, feed the hungry, work for justice, do unto others as you would have them do unto you, practice kindness, caring, compassion, love, peace.

How did "pro-life" get obsessed with life of the fetus, incapable of seeing other "life": mothers, women, animals, trees, all sentient beings and the incredible biodiversity of life on this earth? How did critical thinking, history, music, art, curiosity, science, questioning, inclusion, diversity become "Woke" — censored, banned rather embraced as our path to deeper understanding of self and world?

And how does hate turn so beautifully into joy and love? It is possible!

August 28th, 2023
Choose truth, democracy, life

I think of good people trying to protect and help friends from following a path destructive to themselves, their family, their community: friends suffering from addiction, alcoholism, mental illness, violence. In "intervention" people confront a person's denial, naming the dangerous behavior, hoping friends are able to see and change. Out of love, they try to heal.

I think also of how groups can do the opposite: spread hate. Like a virus, a poison. When I hear a group laughing at Trump's mocking of someone with disability, cheering him when he demeans someone, I think of Orwell's "herd poisoning." I'm dismayed that, with few exceptions, "leaders" of the now Republican Party — in the Senate and House, along with our local senators, representatives, and legislators — say nothing when Trump behaves in despicable, dangerous ways, his words stirring "people" to violence against anyone daring to challenge his autocratic power. How they support even cheer Trumps' tirades, words and behavior, behavior we would never tolerate in our child, spouse, father, neighbor. Our Stefanik remains totally faithful in her support of Trump, viciously attacking truthtellers with inflammatory accusations. Stec and local north country Republican legislators stay silent. For some it's fear of Trump's threats and violence. With Stefanik, it's power, her wanting power. With his "base" it seems a wilful ignorance about facts or evidence, a dangerous and extreme loyalty to a man who would be king. The comradery, the laughter, the cheering…of what is mean and hurtful.

I fear how poisons spread so easily and do so much harm.

September 18th, 2023
Less political polling, more understanding

In my entire life neither I nor any people I know have been "polled" about our views. I am sick of obsessive continuous polls comparing Trump or Biden or about Biden's age instead of examining what candidates say, value, and do.

We should be asked what we value as individuals, a country, a world–ask ourselves to reflect deeply not repeat soundbites. Don't most of us feel that earth, our home, must be sustained, preserved for us, our children, and all beings? Know it's wrong to pollute rivers, water, air, creating toxic neighborhoods? Don't we feel pain when others — in another part of our country or in other countries — suffer climate catastrophes such as floods, fires, droughts? When we hear about deaths of loved ones, aren't we traumatized by needless violence, want sensible gun control? Don't we feel pain of young girls raped, of women living in states where people report them

for crossing a state line to access health care, where doctors fear arrest for saving lives? Aren't many burdened by prescriptive drug costs and Big Pharma profits? Isn't extreme income inequality wrong, harmful to democracy, corrupting politicians rather than serving their community? How could we not support raising the minimum wage, creating affordable housing, supplementing prohibitive costs for childcare?

Most of us want what's fair and just, respect honesty and integrity, are fed by real debate about issues. It's true some are addicted, obsessed with greed, wanting more for themselves, willing to harm another for power. Some, out of fear or hatred, want control over others, casting out all who make them uncomfortable. But most people, I believe — or choose to believe — recognize the power of honesty, kindness, caring, recognize our connection to each other and to our earth.

October 7th, 2023
Freedom Caucus should refocus their attention

The House "Freedom Caucus" — Greene, Bombart, Gaetz — strut around, wielding power, threatening McCarthy, following Trump's command to close government down no matter the cost. Instead of meaningful legislation, the House began impeachment procedures against President Biden, their four "star witnesses" admitting no evidence of criminal actions. Meanwhile they're silent about the four indictments and 91 charges against Trump—overwhelming evidence of fraud, interference with elections, lying, rousing violence, attempting to overthrow our democracy.

Meanwhile Trump threatens anyone speaking truth— journalists, judges, Republicans, Democrats, Biden, Garland, jurists, the justice department, election officials, Milley — all needing security guards protecting them from the violence stirred by this former president who feels the Constitution gives him the right to do whatever he wants.

Biden defined democracy as "rule of the people...respecting free and fair elections, adhering to the Constitution...protecting and expanding rights with each successive generation." But Republican Legislatures in 31 states have introduced legislation not expanding but restricting voting: limiting access to mail-in voting, increasing or imposing voter ID requirements, consciously gerrymandering districts to consolidate power. They pass draconian restrictions on abortion and dismiss heart wrenching calls for gun restrictions. Yet a majority of their citizens want abortion rights, gun restrictions, bipartisan districting. Wisconsin and North Carolina, each evenly divided between Republicans and Democrats, created rigged maps giving Republicans control of two thirds of the seats in the legislature, a veto-proof majority. Clearly "state's rights" are "rights" for power, not people.

Governor Hochul signed legislation making voting by mail more accessible. Stefanik and state Republicans sued, declaring her actions unconstitutional, "destroying election integrity," But what destroyed integrity was Trump's tirade about the "stolen election," endorsing only election deniers. I'm horrified at lies, people yelling "wok," idiots banning books, bullies threatening. I can't understand good people worshiping cruel demagogues, not caring about democracy and our sustainable liveable earth.

October 26th, 2023
Terrorism thrives on hatred, violence and ignorance

Terrorism exists at all levels, making us afraid: ISIS, Hamas, war lords in Sudan and the Congo, men with guns everywhere killing innocent people; bombs destroying homes, lives; dictators repressing, killing, imprisoning journalists and those wanting democracy; Taliban restricting girls from education, women from work. In our country, election workers, librarians, teachers, judges threatened for doing their jobs; politicians threatened when they don't bow before Trump, don't elect Jordan (his pick for House leader). Bork, a Conservative Republican: "I've had four death threats, been evicted from my office…and everybody is getting family members threatened…"

I think of Trump and Netanyahu, two "leaders" caring nothing for their country, only for themselves. Rather than responding to people's real needs for good work, dignity, a living wage, affordable housing, affordable health-care, a liveable biodiverse earth, Trump demands total loyalty. Netanyahu, like Trump, surrounds himself by loyalists, corrupt right wing politicians who, in earlier years, were condemned for their racism, Now in power they attempt to limit the Judiciary, keep Netanyahu from jail, and protect violent Israeli settlers in their attacks against Palestinian homes, farms, trees, refusing to recognize Palestinian rights and the possibility of peace.

The conflict isn't between different religions, races, genders; it's when one religion, one color, one gender feels itself superior, feels it's their natural right to dominate. Christian Extremists wage their cultural wars, attacking women, gays and trans, enacting discriminatory laws. White supremacists attack Blacks, Jews, Moslems; male supremacists view domestic violence and misogyny as their natural right; and corporations use their power to remove regulations protecting air and water and establish laws protecting their huge profits over our liveable sustainable earth.

Terrorism thrives on hatred, violence, fear, ignorance, silence. Our struggle must be to affirm the possiblilty and necessity of love, peace, beauty, bounty, diversity, justice and the reality of the interconnection and interdependence of all beings.

November 22nd, 2023
Trump's troubles are flights of fancy

Trump lists enemies he will "root out": "Communists, Marxists, Racists, and Radical Left 'Thugs' that live like vermin within the confines of our country, lie, steal, and cheat on elections and will do anything possible, whether legally or illegally, to destroy America and the American Dream… Despite the hatred and anger of the Radical Left Lunatics who want to destroy our country, we will make America great again."

What's he talking about? What evil programs of "radical left lunatics"? American Rescue Plan, Infrastructure Bill, Chips and Science Act, Inflation Reduction Act?

A growing healthy economy, high employment, manufacturing returning, household wealth increasing, higher wages, money for our communities (broad band, bridges, infrastructure…).

What "evils"? Lowering cost of prescription drugs; unions organizing and winning.

What do these "lunatics" want: Increasing taxes on corporations and the wealthy, fixing tax loopholes'; child tax credit, subsidizing child care; banning assault weapons; protecting voting rights; protecting air, water; women controlling their own bodies; incentivizing green energy, divesting from fossil fuels, climate justice, protecting our earth..

Were I living in Germany in the late 1930's, I'd be one of Hitler's/Trump's "vermin," rounded up as a Jewish liberal activist fighting for earth, democracy, justice.

Trump, Stefanik, and MAGA scream their "grievances" — projecting onto Democrats crimes they themselves commit: lying, stealing, cheating on elections.

They actually laugh at Trump's outrageous behavior, his threats, bullying, laughing at disabled people, at Pelosi's husband having his skull cracked.

If elected Trump promises to surround himself with loyalists — in the FBI, judiciary, cabinet, courts; to arrest dissenters; to round up asylum seekers; to control education; to be a Dictator. I think of Mussolini strutting and millions yelling "El Duce," of the cheering millions saluting Hitler, their Fuhrer, only much much later questioning how they could have followed that madman.

December 30th, 2023
Truth is complex in a complex world

I taught English Composition for 12 years in Great Meadows Prison, a class in how to look closely, examine, define, question, to analyze cause and effect, make connections, to think.

The men wrote deeply, honestly. I gathered together some papers in a book "Breaking Out of Prison: a guide to consciousness, compassion, and freedom," exploring writing as one way to break out of prisons of mind and heart that restrict our thinking and being.

Our human tendency is, often, to not look at what we don't want to see, a willful ignorance–no matter how obvious, how much evidence and facts. We deny our climate crisis, refusing to see dangerous extreme warming, floods, droughts, wildfires, loss of life. We cling to patriarchal power, commit violence against targeted groups, impose Christian right wing extremism — fearful of losing our "privilege" as a man, a white person, a Christian — assuming it's our "natural right" to dominate over another who is not us, not recognizing another's dignity, uniqueness, richness.

 I think of MAGA Republicans, Stefanik, Trump denying what is so obvious: Trump lost the election! He threatens all dissenters, rouses violence and hatred, silences and demeans all who speak truth. His "worshippers" seem able to deny his corruption, cruelty, narcissism, his danger to our democracy, the overwhelming evidence from his former loyalists who pleaded guilty to lying, plotting, creating false electors to steal the election. They "cheer" his clearly stated plans to assume the power of a dictator. They bow to him in ways that are painful, embarrassing. They sell their soul.

Truth is layered, complex. We don't have to relinquish our differences, values, beliefs, but, rather, to listen, allow in new facts and experiences, not cling to the illusion that rigidity and ignorance are "good," that a strong leader/dictator will keep us safe. We can choose to grow into our more authentic and deeper self. The men I taught would often write "Now I see…" An amazing grace.

January 23rd, 2024
Trust the God of love

I think of different "religions" –not difference between faiths (Christian, Jewish, Muslim, Hindu, Buddhist…) but divisions within each faith. On one "side," the voice of love, interconnection, peace, justice; feed the hungry, clothe and shelter the poor, welcome the stranger, break the yoke of injustice, set the oppressed free, beat swords into plowshares. The golden rule. Pope Francis' encyclical about the intricate value of all life, the beauty and fragility of God's creation.

But there is the other side proclaiming the wrath of God, casting out and condemning to hell "sinners" and "infidels, defining the role of girls/women (dress, education, work), declaring abortion a sin, homosexuality an abomination. Those "leaders," those men controlling, as if they were God.

One side: Catholic Workers feed the hungry; Sufis practice peace; Rabbis for Human Rights defend Palestinian land from attacks by right wing attacks by Israeli settlers attacks. Gandhi in India, our Civil Rights movement, the nonviolent struggle for rights, the Hebrew prophets and words of Jesus.

On the other side, hate and violence: the Inquisition (torturing nonbelievers, artists, scientists); the Crusades using violence to conquer, destroying spiritual, philosophical, artistic communities; Ferdinand and Isabel and the Christian monarchy forcing conversion, expulsion of Jews; Jihads, Sunni and Shia killing each other. Expulsion, destruction, extermination of one group by another, each believing "they" are the "true faith." Ideological purity, dogma.

We have a choice: seeing the uniqueness and value of every being and our deep interconnection…Or arrogantly seeing ourselves as superior, condemning, judging, casting out.

"Mama Bears" are very religious Christian women who had believed hateful religious rhetoric, believing their gay or trans sons or daughters were sinful. At some point many "saw the light," realizing their God was a God of love not hate, and that they deeply loved both God and their children. They became loving hugging joyful "mama bears," choosing the religion of love, peace, and goodwill to all.

March 29
The Power of repeated lies

Rereading my letters to the *Post Star*, I see how often I end letters questioning how people could endorse, support, love Trump. I understand greed, the wealthy who want his tax cuts, his removing regulations protecting air, water, health. It's clear white supremacists, antiSemites, and racists know Trump is their man; many Evangelicals and the Christian Right see Trump as savior; and some politicians want power. But how could my good kind neighbors support someone corrupt, cruel, threatening–a dictator who wants total loyalty, promising a "bloodbath" if he loses?

How could they believe Biden and democrats are pedophiles? That Hillary ran child sex trafficking under a pizza parlor? That the election was stolen when 60 court decisions showed no fraud, all evidence indicating the election free and fair, Trump's enablers admitting, under oath they lied? How can you believe our economy terrible when statistics show an economy thriving, wages going up, unemployment low, unions growing, factories and businesses returning to the US? How can you believe that crime and violence have skyrocketed when statistics show crime decreasing significantly. And how declare climate change a hoax when everything around them shows the growing danger: floods, drought, killing heat, warming oceans. Do facts, information, evidence, his violent words, unhinged actions, and support of dictators not matter? Do Democracy, truth, the future generations not matter?

Goebbels, the Nazi propagandist, answers: "If you repeat a lie enough, people will believe it and you will even come to believe it yourself. — A lie told once remains a lie but a lie told a thousand times becomes the truth. It would not be impossible to prove with sufficient repetition and a psychological understanding of the people concerned that a square is in fact a circle. Propaganda must facilitate the displacement of aggression by specifying the targets for hatred."

Trump, Bannon, Stefanik, Miller, Fox News…follow the Fascist script.

April 1, 2024
Immigrants have enriched our country

Immigrants come to our shores "yearning to be free" —escaping violence, persecution, droughts, floods. They enrich our country, working dangerous jobs "Americans" don't want: rail trails, mines, slaughter houses, construction, farms — Chinese, Irish, Italian, from Mexico, Central America, Haiti, Somalia. Towns devastated when factories left, thrived when immigrants were welcomed — children attended schools, new restaurants, stores, health care workers, doctors, nurses, artists, musicians… vibrant diverse communities. But always some rouse hatred and fear against "invasion"—"rapists," "animals," drug users, criminals taking jobs. "The

nonpartisan Congressional Budget Office said: 'No advanced economy is benefiting more from immigration like the U.S." Powell cited "immigration as one of the reasons behind our strong economic growth."

Parents carry children on treacherous journeys, risking lives coming here. Six workers filling potholes in the night died when a cargo ship hit the Baltimore Bridge. All immigrants. A nephew said: "The work he did is what people born in the U.S. won't do. People like him travel with a dream." I think of my father from a small shtetl in Ukraine, his tomato and banana stand in the Bronx, vegetables ripened in a cellar, working outdoors 12 hours a day, 6 days a week. His dream.

We need to protect our border (increased border patrol) and facilitate legal asylum (more counselors, administrators, lawyers). Republicans and Democrats struggled for months creating immigration legislation that could pass in Congress—until Trump commanded House Speaker Johnson to not allow a vote, keeping blame directed against Biden and the "invasion."

Maga wore buttons with photos of a woman killed by an illegal immigrant. Trump said he visited the family. The sister said he never came, only attacked "illegal alien criminals." When a cargo ship struck the Baltimore Bridge many Republicans blamed Biden, infrastructure, Black leadership…. Blaming, attacking, never doing. Biden pledged full economic support, Buttiegieg convened port, labor, and industry creating plans. Biden visited grieving families.

Trump blamed, did nothing.

April 15, 2024
On the grave danger

Trump's lies about a stolen election, name calling, mocking, demeaning, threatening have poisoned our country, unleashing bullying, screaming at teachers, librarians, health workers, threatening violence. He rails about immigrants invading, "poisoning the blood of our country," promises to sweep the nation of immigrants, place them in detention camps, and repeats his script: "We will demolish the Deep state," "drive out the globalists, cast out the Communists, Marxists, and Fascists," "throw off the sick political class that hates our country," 'rout the Fake News Media," "drain the swamp."

What's he talking about? He and Maga are the swamp, his lies are "fake news," he's the tyrant threatening dissenters, wanting total power. He says he'd violate NATO's mutual protection of allies and "encourage Russia to do whatever the hell they want." Maga Republicans have RNC meetings in Hungary, praising Orban's "illiberal democracy," and Tucker Carlson visits Putin. Who are these people supporting dictators? And why isn't the press naming the danger of Trump—instead of obsessively repeating polls and talking about Biden's age?

Trump, Stefanik, Maga… these are our "Fifth Column"—those within a country who aid the "enemy." At the recent CPAC (Conservative Political Action Committee), the right-wing activist Jack Posobiec opened with: "Welcome to the end of democracy. We are here to overthrow it completely. We didn't get all the way there on January 6, but we will endeavor to get rid of it, replacing it with this right here," holding up a cross necklace and saying "After we burn that swamp to the ground, we will establish the new American republic on its ashes, and our first order of business will be righteous retribution for those who betrayed America."

They're clear. What's unclear is how people could vote for those endangering our democracy?

April 20, s024
Who are these People

In the schoolyard there were always some bullies. I would see them strutting around and think (and sometimes say) "who are you, little big shots, bossing everyone around, yelling, threatening, making people afraid." I would see and sometimes say the same words now to our present day bullies – the so called "freedom caucus" who want only freedom for themselves, who challenge every election they lose as rigged, who silence dissent and cast out anyone who does not spout the lie that the 2020 election was stolen or that the violent mob storming the capital were peaceful protestors and innocent hostages. They are the so called "moms for liberty" banning books they've never read, attacking teachers, librarians, election workers doing their good work; they are in the Republican State legislatures demanding their extreme right wing laws be enacted, "inciting fear and stoking anger." Frustrated by their antics, Republican Governor Mike Parson of Mississippi said, "This is unequivocally and without a doubt, the worst show of bad faith I have ever seen in my life."

They claim they're true Conservatives, all other Republicans Rino's. In reality they get their "script" from Trump and those wanting total power, "voting in lockstep in accordance with the message instructions they receive." Some Republican State Legislators frustrated by their antics are fed up with this " small group of swamp creatures trying to destroy institutions for their own selfish ambition": "They have bamboozled people into believing that their fiery rhetoric and their preference for anarchy is conservative…the reality is that they are an obstruction and an annoyance." They are our rabid legislator Stefanik, bombastic Gaetz, conspiracy theorists and Maga Republicans in the House attacking Biden, impeaching Mayorkas, refusing to pass bills that protect our borders, aid Ukraine, or help average Americans. Kowtowing to Trump, the biggest bully in our school yard.

April 1, 2024
Immigrants have enriched our country

Immigrants come to our shores "yearning to be free" --escaping violence, persecution, droughts, floods. They enrich our country, working dangerous jobs "Americans" don't want rail trails, mines, slaughter-houses, construction, farms–Chinese, Irish, Italian, from Mexico, Central America, Haiti, Somalia… Towns devastated when factories left thrived when immigrants were welcomed–children attended schools, new restau-rants, stores, health care workers, doctors, nurses, artists, musicians… vibrant diverse communities. But always some rouse hatred and fear against "invasion" – "rapists," "animals," drug users, criminals taking jobs. "The nonpartisan Congressional Budget Office said: 'No advanced economy is benefiting more from immigration like the U.S." Powell cited "immigration as one of the reasons behind our strong economic growth."

Parents carry children on treacherous journeys, risking lives by coming here. Six workers filling potholes in the night died when a cargo ship hit the Baltimore Bridge. All immigrants. A nephew said: "The work he did is what people born in the U.S. won't do. People like him travel with a dream." I think of my father from a small shtetl in Ukraine, his tomato and banana stand in the Bronx, vegetables ripened in a cellar, working outdoors 12 hours a day, 6 days a week. His dream.

We need to protect our border (increase border patrol) and facilitate legal asylum (more counselors, administrators, lawyers). Republicans and Democrats struggled for months creating immigration legislation that could pass in Congress – until Trump commanded House Speaker Johnson to not allow a vote, keeping blame directed against Biden and the "invasion."

Maga wore buttons–photos of a woman killed by an illegal immigrant. Trump said he visited the family. The sister said he never came, only attacked "illegal alien criminals." When a cargo ship struck the Baltimore Bridge many Republicans blamed Biden, infrastructure, Black leadership…. Blaming, attacking, never doing. Biden pledged full economic support, Buttiegieg convened port, labor, and industry creating plans. Biden visited grieving families.

Trump blamed, played golf, did nothing.

It is delusional to refuse to see what is so clear:

The 2020 election was fair and free. 60 court cases, many with Republican judges, all found no evidence of fraud. Yet the litmus test of Trump's power is to make Republican politicians and voters swear the election stolen, selling their integrity to court Trump's favor.

The other delusion, central to our now Republican Party: With record heat, storms, floods, fires, drought, Republican politicians see awareness of the climate crisis as a Democratic ploy, a "hoax." They use their power to limit Biden's programs incentivizing green energy, restricting fossil fuel emission. Recently Ron Desantis, the governor of a state that continually suffers extreme heat and flooding signed a bill striking "climate change" from state laws and banning power generating wind turbines offshore or near the state's coastline. His words: "We're restoring sanity in our approach to energy and rejecting the agenda of the radical green zealots." "Green zealots" who want to protect our earth?

His educational policy follows the same agenda: controlling our ability to see, to think, to question, to understand cause and effect. Laws to control what students read and learn, banning books, restricting curriculum, defining the arts and awareness as "wok."

Another left wing "radical policy" rejected by Republican lawmakers is legislation to "Protect the Vote," the cornerstone of democracy, making voting accessible to all people, having election maps drawn fairly, and getting dark money out of politics. Sometimes buying politicians is pretty obvious. Recently Trump had a millionaires' dinner party where he presented a "deal." He would reverse dozens of Biden's environmental regulations aimed at halting the catastrophic advance of climate change by allowing unlimited drilling, adding billions of tons of carbon, if they gave him one billion dollars. In other words, he would sell our earth, and their greed would destroy our earth. He would also lower their already low taxes.

Polls say people care only about inflation–which, actually, is lower in our country than all other neighboring economies. That we care about violence in the cities (which has decreased) and by immigrants(which is minimal). But the violence I fear is the increase in domestic violence (against women) and terrorist violence (stirred by racial hatred); the violence against election workers, teachers, librarians, nurses, protesters and all those threatened when they speak truth. And, most deeply, I fear the loss of truth, democracy, and our precious earth.

Don't sell your soul

Editor:

"Don't give or sell your soul away cause all that you have is your soul... Hunger only for a taste of justice, hunger only for a world of truth" – a song by Tracy Chapman.

I think of Trump, his "deal" at a dinner organized by oil billionaires. For a mere billion dollars he would reverse dozens of Biden's environmental regulations aimed at halting the catastrophic advance of climate change – floods, droughts, wildfires, intense storms, record heat, warming ocean. His "deal" would add four billion tons of carbon by 2030 resulting in $900 billion dollars in damages from climate disasters. Loss of homes, of lives, of hope. Trump said, he would also lower their taxes. In other words he would sell our home, our earth, for greed and power. Not only earth but democracy.

MAGA Republicans praise Putin and Orban, echo their words, bow before Trump's dictatorial commands, repeat his lies: the election stolen, the press rigged, judges all corrupt, his crimes a witch-hunt. Trump threatens all dissenters, uses language we wouldn't allow our children to use, promises to free Jan. 6 insurrectionists, arrest protestors, throw out millions of undocumented immigrants, put his people everywhere – no checks, balances, guardrails. A dictator.

MAGA, including Stefanik, praise him and viciously attack, blame, accuse honest people trying to do their honest work. I think of those who hunger "for a taste of justice" and a "world of truth" – risking their lives to protect biodiversity, save the Amazon, protect old growth forests, coral reefs, endangered species, oceans, rivers, streams, those working to protect citizens from toxins in water and air, from injustice, from poverty–indigenous peoples, whistleblowers, journalists, teachers, scientists, poets, doctors, workers, farmers doing regenerative agriculture, parents who want a livable earth for their children... so many people protecting life and what is precious, saving their soul.

Bernice Mennis

183

June 3, 2024
On inclusion, exclusion

I went yesterday to our Glens Falls Gay Pride Celebration at City Park. It was filled–with families, children, all kinds of people in all kinds of outfits enjoying each other, dancing, listening to music, having a good time. And I thought: why do some people hate certain people for no reason, people who are not doing harm but just trying to live their authentic lives. Why do some people teach their children hate and why do some preachers rant about abomination, sin, damnation. I thought of all the groups targeted for hate throughout history: Blacks, Jews, gays and lesbians, trans, immigrants, people with different abilities, indigenous peoples…People who we enslaved, who inhabited the land we stole, people whom we exploited, people we oppressed–seeing ourselves as superior, seeing them as objects, as savages, as lesser, never learning all they knew, all they could teach us about the earth, about other ways of seeing and being, lessons learned from their lives, their struggles. Yesterday i thought what it means to include, rather than exclude, to widen our circle of learning, wisdom, life….to take in rather than keep out. How fear of "the other" makes us do terrible things to others without feeling any remorse, thought how connected fear is to hate and how hate shrinks hearts, minds, lives–all that effort to hate, to not see, to keep out, diminishing our possible world. I think of my new bumper sticker: "I'd rather be excluded for who I include than included for who I exclude. "Imagine the freedom, the joy, welcoming the "other" and also welcoming and loving all the parts of our own deeper (and sometimes rejected) self.

I thought of my other bumper sticker: "When the power of love overcomes the love of power, the world (and we) will know peace."

Letter, to the Chronicle, addressed to their editor Mark Frost

Mark, I read your "Stefanik's devastating blow to the Ivory Tower." What I saw was a self-righteous opportunist attacking, demanding a yes or no answer from ivy league presidents on whether they support the "genocide of Jews." No students called for genocide of Jews. It's not anti-Semitic to support Palestinians, want a cease fire, speak against devastating loss of life. We should all condemn genocide against any peoples and condemn terrorism in all forms: the violence of Hamas, racist Israeli settlers attacking innocent Palestinians living in the West Bank, domestic terrorists here attacking those they hate.

I'd like Stefanik to answer yes or no to the following: Did Biden win a fair and free election? Did Trump deny the results, set up fake electors, attempt to overthrow democracy? Did she take credit for Biden's Covid relief, infrastructure, inflation reduction act – all bringing money to our community – legislation she voted against? Did she support Paladino with his anti-semitic and racist statements and continue to support election deniers? Did she condemn the Alt right's anti-Semitic "Jews will not replace us," and Trump" calling them "fine and good people".?

I, too, have questions about elite schools, but not her questions: high cost of tuition, legacy admissions, not giving scholarships based on low income. I question the growing disparity between the rich and the poor and the incredible power of the rich to shape legislation. Does she question fossil fuel companies about their emissions threatening life on earth, about what they knew, what they hid? Does she support legislation protecting air, water, earth? Does she question big Pharma's profits and support policies to lower drug costs? Did she vote for lowering taxes on individuals and corporations despite their record profits?

Stefanik went to an elite university. I went to Hunter college for $24.00 a year, city colleges were free then. My Aunt Edith spoke of the "miracle" of immigrant parents who didn't go beyond JHS having children become teachers, doctors, lawyers. Not a miracle, just free four years of liberal arts, the first two exploring what we didn't know: art, herstory (as well as history), black history, workers' struggles, music, philosophy, science, psychology...Not imposed dogma, but questioning, thinking, seeing inter-connections, growing.

Other yes or no questions: should education rouse curiosity, critical thinking, creativity, the excitement of learning? Or should books be banned or burned or censored because they make students (or those in power) uncomfortable? Is discomfort "bad" or a sign that we are growing, "free at last."

POEMS

ON FLAGS AND BUMPER STICKERS

The bright stripes of red, yellow, green and purple
on my peace flag have become dull by years of sun, fain, and snow,
and the large silk banner of earth, suspended
between thin branches and floating in an ocean of blue,
is torn, shredded by constant wind.
I wonder how earth and peace can sustain themselves through the years.

The other day, I took down the old peace flag
and hung a new one by the road.
A small gesture,
especially when the sun shines behind it.
and the wind moves through it.
It flows in the air like water.
Cars pass. I pass.
I am happy seeing it
and the copper heron
spinning with the wind atop our roof,

As for the earth, I need to take it down from the branches
where it hangs, need to find a way to mend
and make whole what has been torn
instead of complain about the harm
that feels beyond repair.

My "Peace on Earth" flag,
a twelve inch square of thick black canvas,
small and unobtrusive, has survived.
Be small and tough perhaps the message.

As for the flags fluttering around our land,
the small Tibetan prayer flags by the campfire
are shredded, thin threads hanging on a string,
diaphanous, transparent, almost invisible in the air,
fragile and beautiful,
like life, like death,
like all our prayers.

My car is another story.
It is strewn with bumper stickers,
splattered with mud.

"Minds are like parachutes, they only function when open"
and "Sow Justice Reap Peace" are still legible,
but "Never have so few taken from so many for so long"
can barely be read, and "Those who can make you believe absurdities
can make you commit atrocities," while true, was written by Voltaire,
an anti Semite, confirming that truth is complex,
and bumper stickers need to be replaced with growing awareness.

Yesterday I put on two new bumper stickers:
"Live Simply that Others may Simply Live" and
"War is Costly, Peace is Priceless."

Well said, I think.

RAISING THE FLAG

Is it a duty,
like the flag of Iceland we raised every morning
in the green mist of fog and rain
to show the way for weary hikers?
Or like flags at military bases, a wave of victory?
Or during war, a symbol of endurance,
vulnerable in battle,
sometimes brave, often arrogant,
in the sun beautiful, flowing like water?

This morning, like every morning,
I go to our peace flag,
a little tattered after all these winters and summers of snow and sun,
bravely waving between two Maples,
but tangled and twisted by last night's wind,
needing to be unfurled,
to be free to wave its colors
no matter the weather.

Suddenly I see myself as one of the ancient ones,
praying each morning for the sun to rise over the distant hills,
our chant welcoming the living sun to warm the breathing earth.
Every morning,
because if we didn't
the consequence too dire
the responsibility too vast,
who would risk?

And of course I know our peace flag
on our dirt road in the Adirondacks
does not save the earth.
But still who is to say what would happen
if I didn't think it my work
to try in every small way, everyday,
to help peace unfurl just a little,
showing anyone who might pass
this possibility of warmth
in this world of cold.

POSTSCRIPT, NOW AT THE END OF THIS JOURNEY

Now at the end of this journey, having reread 21 years of my letters to the editor, this is what I see. I began my letter of October 7, 2002, with "I am writing in love of democracy and freedom and in fear of what is happening now in our country, not about the enemies outside of us but of the danger within us." Now, in 2024, in my last letters, I express the same fear about democracy, but a fear greatly amplified by our present political landscape and by global warming and the climate crisis, the grave danger to our earth, our only home. Reading the letters, I hear how I repeat myself. I write about the continual abuse of power but also the continual courage, goodness, kindness and resistance of so many. I write about the need to open our minds and hearts, to think and feel, to question, to look closely, to speak, to resist, to act. I write about the necessity of defining and redefining our terms, of seeing how easy it is to believe what we are taught and how necessary to question those beliefs: to redefine "cost," "progress," "pro-life," to rethink what is moral and just, who are criminals, what is legal and illegal, what is natural and what a construct of those in power. I write about how important it is to look within ourselves, become conscious of what we value, and I talk about choice, and how we can and must choose the life we want to live and the world we want to live in. I write of my teaching through the years, what I have learned from my students, quote the Bible, Lincoln, the Pope, Martin Luther King, Rabbi Heschel, Einstein, FDR, Eisenhower, Auden, Baldwin… lines from poems and plays, hundreds of my favorite quotes. I look at history – Le Chambon in France during WW2, Nazis coming to power in Germany, at slavery, Jim Crow in the South, our involvement in Central America deposing elected representatives and imposing dictators. I write about FDR's programs, about the Civil Rights Movement. And I write about misinformation and lies…and what we learn much later, and what it means "to finally see."

The people and specific events are different, but the letters of 2002 and 2023 have the same themes: I begin with Bush, the propaganda about Saddam, the lies, the war in Iraq, the loss of so many lives. I write about the power of dark money to influence our legislatures, our laws, our beliefs and understanding, to shape our world...about the rich getting richer, the suffering of the poor...about imperialism, patriarchy, racism and abuse of power…about injustice, voter suppression… I write a lot about our climate crisis, the denial of what is so obvious, our global warming, the drilling, mining, deforestation, the record heat, drought, storms, floods, fires, glaciers melting, coral reefs dying, extinctions, the tipping points, the grave danger to our home. I repeat myself too much because I feel so much so deeply.

In some way nothing has changed at all – the repeated reality of ignorance, greed, and abusive power, the suffering of so many innocents. But now, at the end of 2023, I feel even more the growing danger to Democracy, the Republican Party and Maga now the party of Trump–the danger of his words, his rage, his threats, his violence, his desire for total control and total loyalty – the reality that half of all Republicans are election deniers, and half of Republicans seem to support someone who tried to overthrow our democracy, someone who says, quite clearly, what he would do if he were elected: surround himself with loyalists, arrest dissenters, round up "illegals," take control over different agencies, be a dictator. And I write about the rise of the Christian Evangelical Church and Christian Nationalism, about their movement to ban books, to control curriculum, to control women's bodies

At the end of many of my letters, I write, almost obsessively, of my inability to understand how people–how my good neighbors and kind people in our country –could possibly "choose" Trump, someone so clearly despicable, cruel, narcissistic, so "crazy."

I understand the addiction of greed that makes millionaires want lower taxes and corporations want no regulations of air, water, land, wetlands– anything that would reduce their profits. And I understand the desire for power, Trump, Stefanik, Maga Republicans who will lie, threaten and do anything to keep power, relinquishing any integrity, selling their souls. I can understand fear–those who have been threatened by Trump, who have had to have security around their homes to protect them and their families. I also understand the conscious and unconscious fear of white men afraid of losing their privilege and power–as white, as male. But my kind and good neighbors, how could they support someone so clearly corrupt and cruel as Trump, someone who wants total power and will demean and threaten anyone who threatens their power, how could they cheer and vote for someone so clearly narcissistic and cruel who has given them nothing for their loyalty?

My questions go on: How could they accuse Biden and Democrats of being pedophiles? Think that Hillary ran a child trafficking center under-neath a pizza restaurant? Think that the election was stolen after 60 courts declared the election free of fraud and after the testimony of those who lied admitting their guilt. And how could they believe the economy is terrible when every statistic shows a healthy growing vital economy, low unemployment, rising wages, the growth of unions? How believe that crime and violence have skyrocketed in cities when all statistics show a lessening in violence. In other words, how can people believe what is so clearly untrue?

I thought of Goebbels, the Nazi propagandist, who provided answers to why and how people believe what seems so absurd. His own words: "If you repeat a lie enough, people will believe it, and you will even come to believe it yourself"; "A lie told once remains a lie but a lie told a thousand times becomes the truth": "It would not be impossible to prove with sufficient repetition and a psychological understanding of the people concerned that a square is in fact a circle."; "The essence of propaganda consists in winning people over to an idea so sincerely, so vitally, that in the end they succumb to it so utterly and can never escape from it"; "Propaganda must facilitate the displacement of aggression by specifying the targets for hatred." Exactly. He and now those who want control know what works. The thousands of repeated lies from Bannon, Trump, Stefanik, Steven Miller. Fox New. Tthe people in power and the money in power know the importance of repeating the same script over and over so that "a square is in fact a circle."

I think of the power of repeated lies continually bombarding us, and I wonder about my own illusion or hope or belief that my short letters asking people to observe, question, think, might have some effect. And I wonder how to break through the heavy impermeable wall of lies, misinformation, and rigid belief systems.

I know that love and kindness can change us on a personal level. I think of the mamabears about whom I wrote in one of my letters. Very religious conservative mothers who believed the hateful words of the church about sin, hell, damnation condemning their gay and trans children. Somehow the sad and remorseful words of parents whose homosexual children had committed suicide woke them up, and these mamabears began to see and love their unique children, began embracing a loving God. I think of a white supremacist man filled with hatred of blacks, someone who now goes to schools in Vermont speaking of how dangerous he was and how he changed. He became the sole parent of his small and vulnerable child for whom he felt such a deep love that the hate fell away. And yesterday, at Stewart's, a man mistook me for an older, very kind woman who had befriended him. When I told him about the sweetness of his smile, he said "I was an enraged, violent and mean dickhead." And when I asked what changed him, he pointed to the woman driving and the two little kids in the car and said: "They changed me, their love and kindness."

If lies can imprison us, love and kindness can free us. But I still hope that words can also wake us up, enable us to grow into our deeper selves. With that belief i teach, and I write letters which continue to say: look, think, see, resist, act in this world as if your life depended on it, because it does.

I end with Rabbi Tarfon's comments on Micah 6:8 in the Pirkei Avot:

Do not be daunted by the enormity of this world's grief. Do justly, now. Walk humbly, now. You are not obligated to complete the work, but neither are you free to abandon it.

I have been heartsick and horrified about the loss of innocent lives in Israel, in Gaza, in Sudan, the Congo, Ukraine. Enraged by fundamentalist terrorists, gangs, men with guns kidnapping children in Nigeria, killing and raping women gathering wood. I see the young boys clinging to their mother for safety becoming those men with guns. Continual violence. Tyrants everywhere using their military might to destroy peaceful protests of hundreds of thousands in Belarus, Syria, Hong Kong, Russia…

I think of and repeat Jimmy Carter's words to do what we can, wherever we can, for as long as we can." And I embrace and welcome all that is truly good in our world. I walk in the extraordinary beauty of my Adirondack woodlands in every season, experiencing and actually repeating the words of Hopkins's poem "Nature's Grandeur": "And for all this nature is never spent, there lives the dearest beauty deep down things," feeling a deep gratitude for the beauty of our earth, and for the courage and spirit, the laughter and joy, of so many people who inspire me with kindness, gentleness, hard work and courage.

This Postscript is almost a final letter to the editor–although I know I will continue "letters" and protesting for justice, freedom, democracy, and our earth. Bumper stickers are all over my car: "Tax the Rich," " Live simply that others may simply live," "Critical Thinking the other national deficit." I wear my teeshirts around town: "Feminism is the radical notion that women are people," "Protect our Earth," "Resist," "Fighting tyrants since the Pharaoh." "And in front of our house, on our woodland road, Peace and Earth flags wave in the wind.

I think of the song "Those who believe in freedom cannot rest until it comes."

192

Acknowledgments

Gratitude always to our precious, diverse, bountiful and beautiful earth–trees, woods, spring, streams and mountains which have been my home in the Adirondacks for four decades.

To my four-legged companions and their unique and precious beings who walk everyday in those woods.

To my dear companion, Ann Blanchard, who has created countless pathways in our woods and in my heart, who sees the intricate beauty in nature's many forms, and who was able to whittle my too-long letters to the acceptable 300 words.

To *The Post Star* for persevering and printing the letters – and to all small local newspapers struggling to survive.

To my political comrades in ncea–northcountryearthaction – Lisa Adamson, Diane Collins, Catherine Atherden – for our work together to raise consciousness and create change around the climate crisis and our political crisis: creating a website, giving talks, organizing and joining protests, informing the community of climate events, staging light brigades.

Thanks to Gus Myerberg, who made the lights for our actions. Thanks to Hui Cox who helped me put into acceptable formfor this book the lights showing out actions around town.those lights and actions. And to all those in our community who attended countless rallies and protests, held up lights and flags and signs in every season in every weather.

And to people I would see in the grocery store, laundrymat, on the street, at concerts and movies who stopped to thank me for the letters, inspiring me to persevere, saying that words help us all to continue in the struggle in our own way.

And to my art companions in northcountryarts, all of us knowing how art nourishes our spirit and must be nurtured and protected. And to Sadie Palmer who was able to archive my letters through the years. And Maureen Moore for getting this unwieldy book into form.

And a sincere and deep thanks to all of those in our community and in our country and around the world fighting for justice for all, for lives of dignity, for the preservation of our earth, Their voices, actions, passion, and courage inspire me all my days.

BERNICE MENNIS has lived in and wandered around the woodlands of the Southern Adirondacks for four decades – drawing and painting, writing poems and essays, giving talks and writing workshops, and teaching writing and literature in Great Meadows Prison (for Skidmore College) and in Vermont College's Adult Degree Program (for older students returning to college). She has published two books:*Breaking Out of Prison: A Guide to Consciousness, Compassion, and Freedom,* and *Holding It All,* a book of poetry. Her continual challenge in her life has been to "hold it all" (all our complex feelings) and to break out of the prisons that confine us all in spaces too small for the richness and depth of our lives. This book, *Letters to a Local Newspaper,* allows her to reflect on the politics which have engaged her heart and mind for two decades, reread her too many letters to her local newspaper, and chronicle where she and the world have traveled – to ask questions, make observations, draw connections, and think deeply about our inner values, the outside world, about choices we make, and about the world we want to livein and help shape.

Made in United States
North Haven, CT
05 August 2024

55757203R00109